TALK
STRAIGHT

LISTEN
CAREFULLY

TALK
STRAIGHT

LISTEN
CAREFULLY

THE ART OF INTERVIEWING

M. L. STEIN

SUSAN F. PATERNO

Iowa State Press
A Blackwell Publishing Company

Iowa State Press
A Blackwell Publishing Company
2121 State Avenue, Ames, Iowa 50014

Orders: 1-800-862-6657
Office: 1-515-292-0140
Fax: 1-515-292-3348
Web site: www.iowastatepress.com

Printed on acid-free paper in the United States of America

First edition, 2001

Library of Congress Cataloging-in-Publication Data

Paterno, Susan.
    Talk straight, listen carefully : the art of interviewing / by Susan F. Paterno and M. L. Stein—1st ed.
        p. cm.
    Includes bibliographical references.
    ISBN 0-8138-1838-9 (alk. paper)
    1. Interviewing in journalism.   I. Stein, M. L. (Meyer L.)   II. Title.

PN4784.I6 P38 2001
070.4′4—dc21
                                                            2001016870

The last digit is the print number: 9 8 7 6 5 4 3 2

Contents

Acknowledgments

The authors, in random order, thank the following journalists and authors who took the time to give us their valuable contributions to this book:

Murray Teigh Bloom, freelance
Linda Deutsch, Associated Press
Cindy Yorks, freelance
David Perlman, *San Francisco Chronicle*
Shirley Camper Soman, freelance
David Kaplan, *Newsweek*
Eric Newhouse, *Great Falls* (Montana) *Tribune*
Sue Russell, freelance
Joseph L. Galloway, *U.S. News & World Report*
Joan Acocella, *The New Yorker*
Charles Bartels, Associated Press
Paul Grondahl, *Albany* (N.Y.) *Times Union*
Arline Inge, freelance
Dan Hurley, freelance
Fran Carpentier, *Parade*
George Varga, *San Diego Union-Tribune*
Bill Nottingham, *Los Angeles Times*
Harold W. Fuson Jr., *Copley Press*

Eric Nalder, *investigative reporter*
Mike McGraw, *Kansas City Star*
John Sawatsky, best-selling nonfiction author
Michael Stanton, *Providence Journal-Bulletin*
Bill Malinowski, *Providence Journal-Bulletin*
Pat Stith, *Raleigh News and Observer*
Bill Gloede, *Editor & Publisher*
David Levine, *Tribune-Democrat,* Johnstown, PA.
Matt Coker, *OC Weekly*
Don Ray, investigative reporter
Sheila Ann Feeney, feature writer

We also wish to thank Investigative Reporters & Editors at
the University of Missouri School of Journalism for its contribution to this book.

TALK STRAIGHT

STRAIGHT

LISTEN
CAREFULLY

1

The Need for an Interview and How to Get One

People talking to each other is the essence of journalism and several other fields. Professionals of all kinds rely on an interview for obtaining information. A doctor interviews a patient. A social worker interviews a client; a job applicant is interviewed by an employer. A police officer questions a suspect or a witness, and a taxpayer quizzes the IRS on how to prepare his return. Their aim is to extract essential knowledge to help them come to a decision or to help the interviewee.

In journalism, quotes—or the lack of them—can make or break a story. Neal Shine, former publisher of the *Detroit Free Press,* recalled at a Freedom Forum conference that during his early years on newspapers, a young reporter was sent out to cover a major fire. In phoning in his account to a crusty rewrite man, the novice described the blaze with a stream of overheated adjectives. The older man cut him off, barking: "I know what flames look like . . . Get me some quotes." The rewrite man knew that almost any story, particularly one like that, requires quotes to make it come alive for the reader.

Interviewing is usually the first step in non-fiction writing. For the journalist, the ability to interview is often the critical element in putting together a news or feature story or broadcast. By talking to information sources, she can get facts that give life and meaning to the story. An individual may also be asked to refute or confirm charges against him, thus providing balance and fairness to an account. The interviewee might be able to fill in gaps left after a reporter has plowed through records and newspaper clips, or milked other sources. A story may be impossible to write without the context issuing from sources. Journalism is not fiction. You must have facts.

Investigative reporter Eric Nalder suggests that reporters imagine a successful interview before it actually takes place. "Reporters who don't believe they will get the interview or the information usually fail," he adds. "As far as I'm concerned, no one should ever refuse to talk to me. It works."

An interview also can add color and variety to a story with startling or funny quotes, which may wind up in the headline. Examine the editorial content of any newspaper or news magazine and note how many stories involve interviews. How many broadcasts have you seen in which subjects are interviewed, whether it be straight news, sports, or entertainment? Generally, it's unthinkable that a reporter would start typing a news or feature story or go on the air without having interviewed anyone. Even public relations handouts usually require getting in touch with one or more sources before a story is written or aired.

Moreover, interviews lend credibility to the story. Readers or viewers are likely to put more faith in a report in which sources close to the story are presented. A story about a labor dispute, for example, would be weak indeed without talking to representatives of management and the union. The same goes for reports on disasters, foreign relations, racketeering, schools, lifestyles, and a number of other subjects. The reader or viewer is apt to place more confidence in a report when he hears it from the "horse's mouth." This doesn't mean he or she will automatically accept a statement as truth, but at least it gives them something to evaluate. Joseph L. Galloway, senior writer for *U.S. News & World Report* and a noted foreign correspondent, states: "Interviewing is one of the most personal and valuable of the people skills you must have or acquire, if you are to be a good reporter."

Getting the Interview

Obtaining an interview can be hard or easy, depending on various factors. An individual involved in a crime or an investigation may be a difficult target. Parents whose child has been arrested, hurt in an accident, or murdered will often shun the media. An executive whose company is rumored to be planning a merger with a major corporation wants to duck reporters until the deal is done and is not concerned over your desire to get a scoop. A $30 million lottery winner may not be anxious to spread word of his good luck for fear he will be besieged by scam artists—or an ex-spouse.

On the other hand, any number of newsmakers will put out the welcome mat for reporters, including some lucky lottery players. They include politicians, attorneys, new-product developers, foundation officials, law enforcement officers (sometimes), and almost anyone with a cause to promote, a complaint to make public, or a warning to issue in the general interest such as the onset of the flu season. Media organizations often will receive invitations to news conferences or public relations handouts making available spokespersons for one-on-one interviews. An interview with the author of a new book is usually a slam-dunk. He and the publisher want as much exposure as possible. A newspaper city editor or broadcast assignment editor must winnow out those with the best possibility for a usable story since it's virtually impossible to cover them all. P.R. writers soon learn their releases must have real news or feature value to avoid the trash can, where many of them land.

But let's concentrate for a moment on the sources who are not so readily available and actually may be trying to avoid the media. Your first thought may be to find the person's number, pick up the phone, and simply call him. It's a good thought and it sometimes works—particularly if there isn't a battery of secretaries and other aides blocking your way. Assuming you're prepared for the interview, identify yourself, state the reason for the call, and ask for an appointment. If he balks or hesitates, be politely persistent. Editors are not kindly disposed to reporters who draw zeroes for their efforts. Assure the individual he can select the time and place of the interview—within reason, of course. Deadlines can't be stalled. If the meeting can be to his benefit, emphasize the point. But be honest. In many instances, the benefit falls on the reporter, the news organization, and the public—not the sources. Finally, if a rendezvous is out, try and do the interview on the phone. Telephonic interviews and tough barriers will be discussed in subsequent chapters.

Recalling his years as a reporter and columnist, former *Los Angeles Times* City Editor Bill Boyarsky says he spent as little time as possible on the phone, pushing instead for a face-to-face meeting. "I would say, 'I know you don't want to talk to me but let me come over anyway. I'll explain what I want and if you still don't want to say anything, I'll leave.' It worked almost every time. I was dressed nicely and was polite. I believe in treating sources the way I would want to be treated."

The most dramatic example of his success, Boyarsky remembers, occurred during his interview with the police chief of Los Angeles, who had started a drug rehabilitation program.

"It was known that the chief's son was a drug offender but the chief had never talked publicly about it," Boyarsky relates. "I was under orders from my editor to bring that subject up. I knew I had to phrase the question very carefully so I started out by saying, 'We've all had drug problems in our families. Does your son's problem with narcotics have anything to do with your belief in this program?' 'Yeah,' he replied. And then he talked nonstop about his son."

Going Around End

Alas, obtaining an interview is often more complex than making a direct phone call. There are untold scores of sources with unlisted numbers, reclusive domiciles, day and night protectors, and a deep fear and/or antipathy regarding reporters. The late eccentric multimillionaire Howard Hughes moved constantly to avoid the press—and most everyone else. Actress Greta Garbo became better known for her "I want to be alone" plea than for her movies. Currently, certain celebrities have a frigid attitude toward interviews, including actors Dustin Hoffman and Al Pacino, Minnesota Governor Jesse Ventura, former first lady Nancy Reagan, and all of the Supreme Court justices.

Then there are others who may not have a built-in aversion to being interviewed, but various factors such as the demands of their job, their shyness, or the protective wall set up by their assistants can create a tough challenge. Occasionally, the boss is not even aware of the wall and would be quite easily accessible if approached directly.

In any event, the wall must be breached. None of the top investigative reporters of our time, including Bob Woodward and Carl Bernstein of Watergate fame, would have achieved their successes if they had given up on attempting to reach key sources. The late Ed Montgomery, a Pulitzer Prize-winning reporter for the *San Francisco Examiner*, would work the phone for hours until he contacted the persons necessary to his story, no matter how mighty or lowly they were.

Obviously, getting to your source directly is the best approach. When you're on a deadline it saves valuable time. But this isn't always possible. He may not be taking calls or is away from his office or home, forcing a new stratagem. One alternative is to attempt to reach subjects through their friends, associates, secretaries, spouses, ex-spouses, public relations reps, or anyone else who may provide a pipeline to the individual. If they can't set up an interview for you, they may at least give you an unlisted phone number or inform you where he usually spends his weekends. Also, one or more of your colleagues in the newsroom may previously have covered the person and knows the best way to contact him. Moreover, your office's files may yield a clue or two.

Cultivation of secretaries is a time-honored practice in connecting with important people. Treat them nicely. Don't throw your weight around, for example, "I'm from the *Daily Thunder* and I want to see your boss right now." That will get you to the street door in a hurry. Be polite in your request. Sometimes a complimentary remark about the secretary will ease your way in. Some journalists have showered candy and flowers on cooperative secretaries. This may not work but, if necessary, turn on the charm.

Never assume an interview is impossible because of the position or status of the subject. *Washington Post* reporter James Grimaldi obtained an interview with Federal Judge Thomas Penfield Jackson just after he issued his momentous ruling calling for the split-up of Microsoft Corporation. Aware that interviews with judges are very difficult to get under any circumstances, a CNBC anchor asked Grimaldi how he was able to manage it. "I asked him," the newsman replied. Don't forget the direct approach before seeking more roundabout solutions.

The P.R. Link

Public relations practitioners are held in low esteem by some journalists, who consider them a hindrance to gaining factual information. They're regarded as mere apologists for their employers, obfuscating or distorting the truth when tough questions are asked. Unfortunately, the accusation is accurate for a minority of P.R. people. Most of them, however, try hard to help a reporter fashion a story and that effort is appreciated. The element to keep in mind is that public relations personnel are paid by their employers to present a favorable image of a company, institution or individual to the public. In short, they don't go out of their way to damage that image. Professional spokespersons of integrity will give out information they're allowed to release and be candid about what they can't disclose or don't know. In some cases, they will offer to try to obtain missing facts. At the Camp David peace talks in 2000 between then-Israeli prime minister Ehud Barak and Palestinian leader Yasser Arafat, a news blackout was in effect. Presidential press secretary Joe Lockhart told the media what he could, which wasn't much. However, leaks sprang from Israeli and Palestinian sources that allowed reporters to flesh out the story. The fact that the two sides and former President Bill Clinton met for several hours is not the stuff that makes an editor's pulse race. It's not hot news.

A savvy P.R. person can convince a media-scared superior that it's in his best interest to issue a statement, hold still for an interview, or even agree to a news conference. When the famed Los Alamos and Lawrence Livermore national laboratories came under fire in 2000 in the wake of security scandals, a public relations blitz ensued. While officials of the facilities admitted lapses and vowed to correct them, they also admonished Congress and the Energy Department for interference they asserted did more harm than good. In a *Los Angeles Times* story, Houston T. Hawkins, the security director of Los Alamos, charged that this "incessant negative body-slamming of this institution is harming the national security." Richard C. Atkinson, president of the University of California, Berkeley, which administers the labs, contended that the university did not need them for its survival, "But I don't think the nuclear labs and the whole defense establishment can survive without the scientific leadership the university provides." These officials were most likely prodded to speak out.

The Request Is in the Mail

In the early part of the last century, United States presidents conducted press conferences and interviews by directing reporters to submit their questions in advance. Of course, this provided a president the privilege of culling only those queries he thought safe and self-serving, dumping those he deemed embarrassing.

Presidents don't do that anymore (although they may ignore a hostile reporter's raised hand at a news conference), and neither do most public figures from whom you are likely to seek interviews. Still, when phone calls and other tactics fail, you might try sending the subject a letter, e-mail, or fax explaining your objective and even posing one or two key questions you intend to ask. State the name of your publication or broadcast outlet, your title, and the name of the editor who gave you the assignment. If you have interviewed other people your source might know, mention it. In this type of situation you need all the credentials you can muster. You might also give assurances that you would be willing to discuss any request she may have for off-the-record information. But tread carefully here. If her ban goes to the heart of your story, the interview will be only an exercise in frustration. On the other hand, if she wishes to omit a few details of, say, a former relationship, there's no harm in agreeing. Naturally, she doesn't have to reveal anything about the connection, but many things are said in an interview that, although not important in themselves, help put the main matter in proper context.

In your message to the source, be sure to include your office, cell, and home numbers, making it clear she can call anytime. If you don't get a reply within a few days, phone again to learn whether she got the missive. If so, press your point. Persistent journalists usually get what they go after. Georgie Anne Geyer, a prominent foreign correspondent and columnist for Universal Press Syndicate, acquired her reputation for doggedness early in her career. She was covering a guerrilla war against the government in Guatemala and was trying to make contact with underground leaders. When her initial efforts fell short, she trekked into dangerous mountain country, found the rebel leader, and interviewed him. Her articles on the encounter were published around the world. She used the same determination later to interview world figures such as Cuban president Fidel Castro, Palestinian leader Yasser Arafat, Iraqi dictator Saddam Hussein, and Iran's Ayatolla Khomeini. Sometimes both patience and imagination are necessary to obtain an interview. In his book, *Coups & Earthquakes,* famed AP foreign correspondent Mort Rosenblum recalls that reporters were having no luck interviewing the then-foreign minister of Uganda until they learned he owned a nightclub just outside the capital. By getting a dance partner, they could go to the club, where they found him readily available and willing to talk.

As a matter of survival, experienced journalists have developed strategems for getting interviews that do not fall into their laps. A luncheon speaker must dash off to catch a plane right after his talk and can't hold still for a needed questioning to expand on some of his remarks. Accompany him to the airport, even offering to pay the cab fare. A 30- or 40-minute ride should enable you to round out the speech. A junior high school teacher is willing to tell what he knows about dope-sellers on the campus but he won't discuss it on school property. Fine. Set up a meeting at a restaurant or at his home—or at your office. A source is adamant about not being interviewed—anywhere. If he won't budge, inform him that he will be in the story anyway so he may as well speak out to counter possible negative appraisals of him. In another situation, a mid-level employee in the city's water department says all statements must come from her supervisor, who won't issue any comment about complaints of foul-tasting water. Assure the source that her identity will be protected. In short, be prepared to overcome any obstacle in the way of an interview.

You Don't Have to Be an Expert

If you hold a Ph.D. in physics and have journalistic skills, you are probably an ideal person to interview a famous physicist on a scientific breakthrough. Similarly, a reporter who is an ex-priest will likely know the right questions to ask an Archbishop.

But expertise, however welcome in the newsroom, is not necessary to interview experts. A journalist can easily educate himself on a particular subject so that he can ask intelligent questions of a source whether he or she be an aerospace engineer, football coach, psychologist, college president, horse trainer, or software developer. Success lies in boning up on the subject or source to enable you to ask intelligent, probing questions.

Allan R. Andrews, executive news editor for *The Stars and Stripes,* is convinced that "journalism remains a field for the last generalists." Writing in *The American Reporter,* Andrews challenges assumptions that only those with proper backgrounds can write about esoteric subjects. "Must one be a pilot to write about airplanes?" he asks. "Build computers to report about them? Practice medicine to write about healing? Be a parent to write about child care. . . ?"

To Andrews, the answer is clearly no. "One of journalism's attractions is the constant learning," he emphasizes. "A reporter assigned to cover a carnival must learn the ways of carnivals."

Pulitzer Prizes and other journalism awards have been won by reporters who began projects with little or no knowledge of the subject. They learned on the job or did extensive research.

Eventually, you may want to specialize in politics, science, the arts, entertainment, or finance. At that point, you will, indeed, become the newspaper, magazine, or broadcast station's expert in that area and will be respected by sources, editors and your audience alike. Meanwhile, be assured that respectability also falls on top-notch general assignment reporters.

2

Preparing for the Interview

Before you arrange for an interview, prepare. Ask yourself: What's my story about? How will I focus my reporting? Try to boil down your story idea to one or two focused sentences that illuminate the issue, problem, or controversy. Then make a list of people you need or want to interview. To figure out who those people might be, ask yourself more questions: Who are the main characters in my story? What are they doing? Who are their critics? What are the names of experts who can provide facts and evidence to explain questions raised by the main characters and their critics? Which government or regulatory officials might provide facts or evidence to support the claims of supporters or opponents? Finally, remember to interview average, everyday people who are affected by the problem or controversy.

The "key is to be very prepared," says Bill Nottingham, a high-ranking editor with the *Los Angeles Times*. When he was working as a reporter, Nottingham remembers he would write out questions ahead of time, "and note how I might follow up if the person answered 'Yes' or 'No.' Plus, I always tried to toss in a question I already knew the answer to, so I could test the source's truthfulness."

Once you've got a story idea, seek out supporters, opponents, and experts. Go to the library and search the Internet. Collect all the clips you can find on your subject. "You will conduct better interviews if you broadly research your subjects," says Eric Nalder, a Pulitzer Prize-winning reporter. If you're doing a story about corruption in the provost's office, you better know who the provost is and what one does. Find out everything you can about a particular agency or organization before making a single phone call.

"Find out how the agency or company keeps its records," advises Nalder, then "understand how the system works. Ask questions like: 'When something goes wrong in your agency, where do you write it down?' That will tell you the kinds of documents you need. Ask whether the department conducts audits, and if so, who does them. Contact the people who do the audits and get to know them. Quite often they are concerned about the problems they have discovered in their agency, and they will leak information to you." Whenever you're walking through an office, "get to know the clerks, workers and secretaries. They can often be your best source for documents."

- **Learn the vocabulary and the workings of the office or industry you're writing about.** "I spent a whole year reading *Turkey World* magazine for a series on the department of agriculture," says Mike McGraw, a reporting coach for the *Kansas City Star.* "Gather as many documents—and as much knowledge—as you can." In an ideal world, says Pat Stith, a reporter with *The News and Observer* in Raleigh, North Carolina, "you will know more about a small portion of your source's job—the portion that you intend to write about—than they do. Ideally, our work will have been so thorough we will know the answer to almost every question we intend to ask."

- **Get organized.** Create a source list—in a paper file or your computer. Nalder puts his list on an Excel spread sheet and includes his source's address, office, and home telephone number, as well as other relevant information, such as birthday, social security number, job title, expertise, and so on. "The more people the better," he says. "Don't rule out anybody who might have information that you need. Pick names from newspaper clippings and documents. Ask everyone you talk to whether they can think of other people you should approach. Every time someone says something significant, ask the question, 'How do you know that?'" The answer to that question, he says, often leads to other sources. "Once you have some grasp of your subject, sketch out a plan, even if it is only in your head. Who are you going to interview and in what order? Sometimes you must catch certain people quickly before they're scared off. Other times you must circle them, talking to their friends and associates before you get to them."

- **Collect the evidence you'll need to document provable facts.** While researching the issue, problem, or controversy make sure you collect the evidence you'll need to establish an agreement with your source on basic facts. "Establishing agreement is tantamount to establishing control," says John Sawatsky, one of Canada's premiere investigative reporters and a renowned expert on interviewing. Without agreement, reporters spend most of the interview trying to force sources to accept their version of events, Sawatsky warns, usually resorting to coercion and leading questions.

CBS anchorman Dan Rather illustrates how easily journalists are manipulated by sources in an interview he did
with the wife of former Serbian president Slobedon Milosevic, a member of the ruling party. In the interview, Rather
is clearly trying to confirm that Serbia is behind ethnic
cleansing in Kosovo. Instead of presenting facts about
genocide that his source would have to explain, Rather asks
a series of general, closed-ended questions, and the woman
runs over him like a truck. She answers each question with
a curt denial, followed by a prepared message she wants to
send to the audience, blaming the United States for beating
up Serbia. (See Sidebar 2.1.)

Sidebar 2.1: Show: 60 Minutes
May 2, 1999

If the release of three American prisoners is seen as a softening of
Slobodan Milosevic's attitude toward the United States, there was
nothing soft or even halfway conciliatory in the answers Dan
Rather got during the interview he conducted in Belgrade this
weekend with the woman who was Milosevic's alter ego.

STAHL: If anyone wields power in Serbia other than Slobodan
Milosevic the man who has held NATO at bay for more than a
month, it's the woman he's married to. She is Mirjana Markovic, a
professor of Marxist sociology who serves as her husband's principal adviser. Seldom, if ever, does she meet with Western journalists, and, as far as we know, has never sat down on camera with an
American. But that's just what she did this weekend with Dan
Rather.

As you will hear, she does not give an inch, insists Serbia is blameless, and that the Clinton administration is using the age-old ethnic divisions that have always existed in the Balkans as an excuse to destroy her country.

DAN RATHER: First, thank you for doing this. You have said there are so many things the American people don't understand about this situation. What is it that you think Americans don't understand?

Professor MIRJANA MARKOVIC: First of all, I think that Americans don't know all that they should know in order to understand the situation. During the last months and a few days more, in Yugoslavia and especially Serbia, many children have been killed.

Babies.

Many people were killed, I must say, while they were asleep. I have never seen such a war where people are killed while sleeping. The bombs are falling on schools and nurseries. They are falling on hospitals; one of the first ones destroyed the maternity ward. In Yugoslavia, almost all the bridges were destroyed and a lot of factories, especially the ones that our lives depend upon. A large number of people lost their houses. Our country is close to the point of being destroyed, and I must tell you that I do not believe the American people know all this, and that they approve it.

RATHER: Let me, if I may—this is important—you say that the West and America does not understand what's happening in Kosovo. Is there no ethnic cleansing in Kosovo?

Prof. MARKOVIC: No.

RATHER: None? There are no atrocities committed by Serbs in Kosovo?

Prof. MARKOVIC: No.

No. The Serbs are defending their territory.

RATHER: I ask because you know many witnesses say that the Serbs are doing these things in Kosovo.

Prof. MARKOVIC: I don't believe they did that, and I'm almost sure they didn't do it. I would like to tell the American people that if the American country has some need, which I do not understand, to manifest their great technological and political power, military also, let them manifest it with somebody equal. Let them show the real partner, if they have to do it, but I think that they don't have to do it. Let America be fighting with a partner who is at their technological level. It doesn't make any sense that the American partners in the war should be small, underdeveloped people. American bombs have been falling, as you know, on Somalia, Sudan, Haiti. I must say this is not very courageous. This is if a man who is 40 years old decided to beat up a boy who is 10 years old.

RATHER: How does this end?

Prof. MARKOVIC: The decision is not in our hands, but in yours. We must defend our country the same way as all the countries of the world do it. I do not know a single country which would not protect its own territory—How shall I say it?—when they want to take it away. This decision is not in our hands. We are not bombing anybody. America, which is bombing, and NATO—How should I say?—is under the biggest influence of America—should make this decision.

RATHER: What about the argument, Madam Professor, that the bombing will stop when you, the Serbs, stop killing Kosovar Albanians in Kosovo and stop running them out of their homes, stop killing them?

Prof. MARKOVIC: But they are not killing them. They are not expelling them. This is as if you told me that today is Wednesday, but today is Saturday. If you are talking to me, the elementary assumption is that you believe me. Why should I lie to you? These days, I keep thinking about the poster of an American soldier I had in my room at the university. And this is the famous poster of an American soldier who was killed in Vietnam. And it is written underneath, 'Why?' That was—How should I say?—one of the nicest symbols of the senseless war which lasted many years, and in which many American young men lost their lives. I ask myself, how much time is going to go by before such a poster appears again in America, or somewhere else in the world, with the same 'Why?' but for another reason: 'Why did we kill a small country?'

RATHER: I take—I take the point. This is what makes it even more difficult for Americans to understand what's happening in Kosovo today.

Prof. MARKOVIC: But it is not happening. But it is not happening, what you are saying. And that's why I am taking this opportunity. If you are going to translate everything the way I have just told you, I really wish to send a message to the whole American nation and all the American citizens that the Serbs are not aggressors against the Albanian people. And this is not true. Yugoslavia is defending its territory. Albanians would never have rebelled against Yugoslavia; they would never have wanted to separate form Kosovar territory, if they'd not been encouraged by the outside world. Why should I agree to this conversation if I am not sure of what I am telling you? I did not come to face the whole world to lie.

RATHER: Why did you decide to do this interview? You never do television interviews.

Prof. MARKOVIC: I have never given a television interview. This is my very first interview. Because you convinced me. Because you were so kind, and I trusted you, and because I hope you are not going to deceive me, and that I will not regret for giving this interview. I never give interviews, either in my own country or abroad, because I am afraid of television.

RATHER: But you also feel strongly about the situation.

Prof. MARKOVIC: How couldn't I feel anything? My country is exposed to the most terrible destruction in the second part of the century, maybe in its history.

RATHER: Professor, as I hear you talk, I think you must be aware that there are many people, including many people in the United States of America, but not limited to them, who see your husband, the president, as the new Hitler. This is not the first time you've heard this. And tell me what your reaction is when you hear people say that, say, 'Well, this man, President Milosevic, is the new Hitler.'

Prof. MARKOVIC: I'm reacting in the same way as if you told me that now is the month of January and that we have snow outside, but as you can see, today is the 1st of May, and lilacs are blooming. To be Hitler, he has to fulfill the conditions which would make him Hitler. That means he is the carrier of the organized hatred towards people and the organized violence towards people. My husband doesn't hate any people. He does not use violence. You can believe that. Maybe you will think that I'm not telling the truth; maybe I have deceived you. But I did not. But my husband is not using violence against anyone.

RATHER: It has been written about you that you are your—the president's and your husband's eyes and ears, and that you are his principal adviser. Is this true?

Prof. MARKOVIC: No.

RATHER: You are the power behind the president politically.

Prof. MARKOVIC: No, I am not. I don't accept that I am. I don't accept that I am behind anything. I am a complete person by myself. I take the responsibilities for my shortcomings, and I take all the responsibility for all I think and what I do.

RATHER: Whatever else one may think of Mira Markovic, the wife of the Yugoslav president, Mrs. Milosevic, a reporter comes away from conversations with her convinced that the following things are true: She is, in her own right, a potent political, intellectual and educational force in the country. Number two, television may not fully convey her sense of rage and fury at what she sees as the betrayal of her country by the United States. And also, not everybody here likes her; certainly not everybody agrees with her politically. But what the wife of the Yugoslav president has expressed in this interview does overwhelmingly reflect the view of most Serbians at the moment. To believe otherwise is to kid ourselves.

Rather appears flustered. He gains some control when he asks short open-ended questions—"How does this end?" "Why did you decide to do this interview?"—but loses it again with long, coercive statements, comparing Milosevic to Hitler, for example, or asking, "When will you stop killing Kosovar Albanians?" She beats him back with spin and denial. In the middle of the interview, Rather capitulates, telling her he sees her point when she compares U.S. troops in Kosovo to what she calls "the senseless war" in Vietnam.

Later, on "Larry King Live," Rather blames his source for delivering "one of the strangest interviews I've ever been through. Complete, total denial of provable facts." But Rather never provided Mirjana Markovic with any "provable facts."

If Rather had "provable facts" that Serbia committed ethnic cleansing in Kosovo, he should have questioned the Serbian official about *that evidence,* not about generalities such as genocide.

Without agreement, the journalist spars for control with the source, lurching back and forth between coercive questions and statements. Consider television journalist Roger Mudd's successful strategy to expose problems in Senator Ted Kennedy's first marriage.

At the outset of the interview, Mudd persuades Kennedy to agree to discuss his private life:

> **Mudd:** How fair has the press been to you and your family?
>
> **Kennedy:** They've been fair enough.
>
> **Mudd:** What sort of separation should the press maintain between your public and private life, or any public official?
>
> **Kennedy:** There's a natural inquisitiveness, I understand. . . .

By persuading Kennedy to agree that his personal life is not off limits, Mudd moves from the general to the specific and scores a direct hit with his follow-up question:

> **Mudd:** What's the present state of your own marriage Senator?

So how do journalists establish agreement? By doing as much research about the problem or issue as possible before making a single call to the people who you think will be the main sources for your story. Dan Rather should have had documents or other evidence to show to the Serbian official that would have forced her to respond to particular incidents of genocide he claims were provable. "Research your subject like a prosecutor who wants to win every time," write Connie Fletcher and Jon Ziomek in a *Writer's Digest* article about interviewing strategies.

Sometimes it makes sense to ask the source to provide you with any research materials that might help you. You should also find the best reference librarians in your local or university library and use them often. They'll show you volumes upon volumes of reference books to help you find out about a particular person or subject. They'll also help you figure out how to use the Internet for research; ask them how you can access the library's reference materials from your computer at home. When you've found a few particularly helpful librarians, treat them well and bring them small treats. They will prove invaluable to your reporting.

Once you have the evidence you need to ask intelligent questions, start formulating an angle or hypothesis, a one- or two-sentence focus around which you can begin formulating your interviewing strategies. Once you have the story focus in mind, and you've figured out the people you want to interview to test your hypothesis, how will you begin the interview?

- **Getting started.** The first question sets the tone, so spend some time beforehand thinking about what you want to say. One reporter, assigned to profile a journalist known for her withering interviewing style, started with the question: "If you were interviewing yourself, what would you ask?"

Avoid closed-ended questions, or questions a source can respond to with yes or no. Instead, ask questions beginning with what, how, and why. These open-ended questions will help you understand what happened, how it happened, and why.

Write down the questions you want to ask, then note the crucial questions. If your source cuts the interview short, switch to what you must know to understand the issue or problem. Especially if you're interviewing busy people, you'll want to prepare crucial questions before you pick up the phone to set up the interview.

Celebrities, politicians, public relations people, high-ranking government officials, executives, and professional athletes usually have done so many interviews they come determined to get a particular message across. "If you research well," says journalist and author Carole Rich, "you'll find some tidbit or angle to a story that might lead to an unusual question—and an interesting answer."

Preparation is especially important when you're writing about a sensitive or controversial topic. "You've got to figure you've got one shot," says Pulitzer Prize-winner Michael Stanton, a reporter with the *Providence Journal-Bulletin*. Stanton recalls the time he was doing a story about the biggest corruption probe in Rhode Island's history. One of the star witnesses was an engineer who had bribed state officials for contracts; he had implicated the governor in the scheme. The engineer "wasn't talking to anybody," Stanton says. "We showed up at his office and tried to schmooze him," by saying 'We understand it must be a difficult time for you, we're not trying to get you to re-create testimony, we know about your life and your dealing with the governor.' We softened him up with questions like: 'Is this the couch the governor sat on when he came and talked to you?' We started by asking him for personal information, that led to details about the case, and we were then able to confirm other anecdotes we'd heard."

- **Don't wait to the last minute to call.** "Your schedule must defer to those of your sources," advises Joe Feiertag in *Writer's Digest*. Frequently, when you call busy people, they'll tell you, "I can talk for a few minutes right now." Usually, that means now or never. If you haven't prepared, you'll be in a position to decline the interview, hoping it can be rescheduled (which often it can't) or you'll end up asking uninformed questions.

  "Never start (an interview) with a stupid statement," cautions *Kansas City Star*'s Mike McGraw. "If you're unprepared, really apologize for being uninformed." Appeal to your source's desire to have the story told fairly and accurately. You might say: "Help me understand what happened. I'm not the expert, you are. Because so many thousands of people will read (or see) this, let's get it right." Tell your sources that you'll likely call them back to check your story's facts and to make sure what you've written is accurate. Most sources appreciate that kind of attention to details.

- **Organize your questions.** To keep track of questions, some reporters jot them down on a separate sheet of paper; others suggest writing "single-word clues on the flap of your notebook to remind you of issues you want to cover," says Nalder. "Organize your paperwork so you won't fumble with it as you talk." *The News and Observer*'s Pat Stith says he tags the records he needs to support various questions. "During the interview, if I need a letter or whatever, I can find it quickly. I highlight the critical questions so if (the source) cuts off the interview, I can find them quickly." But, he warns, "Never carry documents out of the office that you can't afford to lose. Nothing with a source's name on it. Or a telephone number. Or a computer printout that might identify the terminal that produced it. Don't show the subject a handwritten letter, even if the tipster is anonymous. He might recognize the writing. Do not make notes in the margin of documents you carry out of the office, as in 'This is BS.' In fact, don't make such notes, period. If you wind up in court, that might be offered as evidence that you made up your mind before you had all the facts."

Before Stith leaves the office, he puts a new tape and new batteries in his tape recorder. And he tests it. He sharpens several pencils and puts a couple of pens in his pockets. "Nothing breaks the aura you want quicker than having to ask the person you're interviewing to loan you a pencil."

Stith offers other practical tips:

Dress appropriately.

Arrive a few minutes early.

Show good manners.

Pick a good seat, as close to the subject as possible, but far enough away so neither the subject nor his associates can see your notes or documents.

- **Inner interviewing.** Both Stith and Nalder practice "inner interviewing." "As a warm-up, maybe during your morning shower, imagine a successful interview," advises Nalder. "Reporters who don't believe they will get the interview or the information usually fail." Stith advises to go to the interview "with all the lights on in your mind. I try to leave my theories about what may have happened back at the office. I want to be open to new facts, and to new interpretations of old facts. As I get out of my car and start into a person's office, I don't think about the questions I intend to ask, or how he or she might respond. I just say to myself, 'Relax and think. Relax and think.' And I say, 'I'm ready. He better be ready.'"

  Nalder continues the technique of inner interviewing as he prepares to meet his sources. Never approach subjects "as though they seem menacing or likely to clam up," he says. "Appear innocent, friendly, unafraid and curious. If you're a hard-boiled, cynical reporter who talks out of the side of your mouth, you'll need acting lessons."

- **Get out of the newsroom.** To find sources—and stories—you need to climb a few stairs. In a piece he wrote for *Editor & Publisher* magazine, editor Bill Gloede seconded the sentiments of a newspaper owner, who says the biggest problem he faces "is getting the reporters off their asses and out into the communities they are supposed to be covering." Says Gloede: "Journalists often like to hang out among themselves, where they may openly proffer their worldviews, even if their job at the moment is to cover East Oshkosh. They often have an open contempt for the people they cover."

"The whole business would be better off if not only reporters, but editors and publishers as well, spent more time in the various communities served by their newspapers. An evening spent sitting around someone's kitchen table, drinking stale coffee and listening to a legion of neighbors armed with bulging file folders sound off about this issue or that can work better than the best promotional campaign at attracting and keeping readers. You also learn what's on their minds. The trick here is for the newspaper people to speak as little as possible. "The press should be a watchdog over government, a skeptical observer of organized pressure groups, an arbiter of nothing, and an ally of the people it serves."

David Levine, editor of the *Tribune-Democrat* in Johnstown, Pennsylvania, remembers the time when one of his reporters took a walk in the park across the street from the newspaper office. "He overheard a conversation between two people mumbling something about layoffs at a local business. He tracked down the mumbling and it resulted in a page one story about a major local business closing," he says. "The point that I keep making with my reporters—young ones, mostly—(is) that you'll never learn anything by sitting at your desks sipping coffee, waiting for the phone to ring. It just doesn't work that way. You have to listen—to people in the park, on the street, at meetings, in stores. Reporters who sit at their desks aren't doing their jobs."

- **Get to know people.** "Don't just call your sources when you want something," says Bill Malinowski, a reporter with the *Providence Journal-Bulletin* well known for cultivating and keeping sources in law enforcement and government. "Get to know your sources. Go running with them. Find out the names of their (spouse) and kids. Call them up to talk about what's in the news or the Red Sox, or anything really, just to talk." Malinowski's penchant for getting to know people paid off in a big way when he received a tip from a couple of officers that the local police chief couldn't locate two kilos of cocaine confiscated in a bust. "I went to the chief, then to the head of internal affairs. They told me it (the cocaine) was either destroyed or in the evidence locker." The reporter gave the department a couple days to find it, and the chief caved: "It was like a surrender. He admitted he couldn't find it." And Malinowski got an impressive scoop.

- **Relax.** "It took me a long time to learn that," says the *Kansas City Star*'s Mike McGraw. "To sit back, relax and look people in the eye." As a young reporter, McGraw remembers how he used to go into interviews with a list of questions. "I'd ask question number one and get the answer. Then I'd ask question number two and get the answer. Then I'd get back to the office, look at my notes and realize the guy didn't answer any of my questions! I was so focused on taking notes and asking the question, I forgot to listen to the answers, to work the questions off

3

What Is Your Objective?

Making your story fair and accurate is your most important objective. To do that, you'll have to interview the right people. If you're writing about a problem or controversy, make sure you've got a list of sources that includes supporters, opponents, and experts. Experts are disinterested observers who can provide objective evidence to help you sort through conflicting opinions and facts provided by supporters and opponents. You should write no single source stories. If the source is the central focus of the story—a profile of someone, for instance—you still have to interview that person's friends and foes.

Go into every interview with a clear goal. Make sure you've discussed the angle and the type of story with your editor. Is it hard news? Feature? News-feature? Profile? Is it 500 words? 5,000 words? Remember, too, that your objective—and your focus—may change as you interview your sources. Be ready to go in any direction that will make yours a better angle, focus, and ultimately, story.

With your story's focus in mind, think about what you hope to achieve in your interviews. Something brought you to this person. What was it?

When you approach people to ask for an interview, say as little as possible, advises investigative reporter John Sawatsky. "Identify who you are, who you represent, what the subject is, and shut up. They may ask questions. Be honest. But don't volunteer information. Make your answers as general as possible without being misleading."

Many journalists prefer interviewing people in person, but doing so "eats up great quantities of time," warns Joe Feiertag in *Writer's Digest*. "Budget according to your time and your story's needs." Consider doing phone interviews first to try to understand the story and its focus. Then, when you have a pretty good idea where you want to go, arrange a meeting.

Reporting by what he calls "hanging around" is one of Eric Nalder's favorite methods. "If you're writing about train wrecks, go to train wrecks. If you're writing about crooked cops, hang out with the cops. It pays to be on the scene."

Once the interview begins—which is as soon as you've identified yourself as a reporter working on a story—never lecture your sources, argue, or debate with them; keep personal opinions and comments to yourself. Keep your anger—or any other emotion besides cheerful interest—in check. Many sources will cut short interviews or refuse to talk to you again if you show bias or behave inappropriately. By maintaining distance and staying in control, you'll avoid having your source intimidate you or put you on the defensive.

Try to make your source comfortable. Begin by lobbing softballs, chit-chatting about your source using questions starting with who, what, when, where, why, and how. Keep the focus on your source. Try to keep your list of questions out of sight. "It's better not to make your subject too aware of the list," advises David Fryxell in *Writer's Digest*. "Gradually, as the conversation warms up, start weaving your questions into the talk. Keep your tone casual. No need to suddenly signal that The Interview is Starting Now."

Sidebar 3.1: Finding Hard-to-Find People

Sometimes the most important interviews are with people who are difficult to find, says investigative reporter Eric Nalder. He offers some tips on finding people:

1. When calling 411 (information) to track down a phone number, list several cities as possibilities rather than one, thus forcing the operator to search an entire area code.
2. Ask your librarian to help you locate a computer or Internet database that provides public records or phone numbers that will help you locate the source. Use birth certificates to get the names of parents and/or other relatives, marriage records, driving records, car licensing records, professional licensing records, divorce records, real estate transactions, records on lawsuits, and criminal records. You can also find out about sources from their property tax records, military records, and old newspaper clippings.
3. Ask a local reference librarian to locate a biographical file on your source.
4. Consult with a private investigator.
5. Interview personal associates of your source. Learn all you can about your target's habits. If she drinks a lot, check the bars where she lives. If she's an avid skier, inquire at skiing organizations or ski shops. Use your

    imagination to consider any and all potential connections.

6. Find the source's former high school or college and ask for the student annual. In there, you'll find names of schoolmates.

7. Obtain a telephone reverse directory—available on the Internet—to get the names, addresses and phone numbers of neighbors.

8. Do a name search on one of the many Internet search engines, especially Yahoo People. If you're unfamiliar with the available search engines, visit your local or university library and speak to a research librarian.

What Is an Interview?

Remember, an interview is not a conversation, says John Sawatsky, a leading expert on the art of the interview. In a conversation, you exchange information. In an interview, you gather information. The difference is subtle, but important. Too many journalists try to browbeat their sources into an admission of wrong-doing, or attempt to seduce them with a single goal in mind: "to lure the subject into saying something he or she shouldn't," writes David Fryxell in *Writer's Digest.* "If the interview is for television rather than print, the ideal seems to be to reduce the subject to tears." Occasionally, you can get people to rise to the bait. But that's the exception. It's also the old way of interviewing, an approach that no longer works. Anyone who has had any experience dealing with reporters has figured out the standard tricks reporters use. In the last decade media trainers have become such a growth industry "you can even find them among small businessmen in Newfoundland," Sawatsky says, teaching politicians and executives "how to run circles around journalists. It's a sophisticated battle for control," he says, with journalists too often relying on outdated, conventional approaches to interviewing.

Sawatsky denounces standard interviewing techniques as "the old methodology," often characterized as a power struggle between interviewer and subject, as a battle of wills, a game to be won or lost. Sawatsky advises changing the framework, taking the mystery out of what most journalists have always believed is a serendipitous experience, likened to "lovemaking" by veteran journalist Claudia Dreifus in a recent book on interviewing.

The conventional method represents an irrational belief "in magic," says Sawatsky. "If an interview goes well, then we say it's magic. But it's not magic. It happens for an understandable reason. It's rational. It's a skill. It's easy to teach someone skills."

Journalists are often trained to appear to be tough by asking accusatory questions, the prosecutorial method of interviewing. Reportorial victories of the previous three decades—the Watergate scandal, the Pentagon Papers, the My Lai massacre—empowered journalists, galvanizing them to ambush and grill unsuspecting sources, who responded with stonewalling or outright hostility. Oriana Fallaci, Mike Wallace and Barbara Walters, took center stage; the source became the enemy to defeat at any cost.

In 1990, Janet Malcolm unleashed a professional tempest when she compared journalists to "a kind of confidence man, preying on people's vanity, ignorance or loneliness, gaining their trust and betraying them without remorse." Malcolm gave voice to conventional interviewing at its worst, and it touched a raw nerve. Based on competition and coercion, the old way often leads journalist and subject to an unavoidable moral impasse. At its best, it leaves information gathering to chance, allowing spin meisters to control what the public learns. In any case, the old way puts journalists in a defensive crouch, attacked by those who believe the media are biased, left-leaning, and agenda-driven. "People are pretty savvy; they know when they're being coerced. And they don't like it. With competition, the goal becomes winning. The more we win, the more they lose. That's a lousy way to get openness. If we thought about it, we'd do it differently," Sawatsky says. "But we don't think, we react."

Interviewing Traps to Avoid

Sometimes seemingly innocuous questions elicit over-the-top responses. That's usually because the reporter has used loaded words, oftentimes without realizing it. In the following example, a reporter begins interviewing media tycoon and business executive Jack Kent Cook with what seems like a reasonable question. But the question angers Cook, he refuses to answer it, and the subsequent questions as well.

> **Reporter:** "What's the biggest mistake you've ever made?"
> **Cook:** "I'm not answering that."
> **Reporter:** "What's your greatest failing?"
> **Cook:** "Failing? Mistake? To hell with my greatest failing. I'm not going to answer that either."

Reporter: "Well then, what's your greatest regret?"
Cook: "Regret? It's the same damn thing, Bob. You can't snare me with that."

The reporter used value-laden, subjective language that offended Cook. If you have to ask a negative question, start first with a positive. "What have been your greatest successes?" After answering the first question, the source will likely be more inclined to answer the second, more negative one. In the course of answering the first question, in fact, the source may allude to a failure. At that point, follow up with: "You mentioned failing. What has been your greatest failing?"

Eliminate subjective values from your questions and the source will feel compelled to fill in the blanks you left behind. Instead of: "Were you surprised?" (surprised is subjective) ask: "How did you react?" Instead of asking: "Did you feel sick?" ask: "How did you feel?" Instead of: "It must have been tough in the early years," ask: "What were the early years like?" The answers become unpredictable. "That's the secret to getting surprising answers from people," says Sawatsky. Questions should arouse the source's need to tell us more.

Sawatsky has spent nearly a decade breaking down interviewing "in much the same way a mechanic would diagnose a troubled car," he explains. After breaking down and rebuilding thousands of interviews, Sawatsky saw patterns. "Interviewing is about people. They're not chemical compounds, and they don't always act predictably. But there is a predictable part." Ask a closed-ended question—one that can be answered with a yes or a no—and sources "will confirm or deny 98 percent of the time," Sawatsky says. "That's the science." The unpredictable part is what happens next. "Socially, people are taught to add a post script to a confirmation or a denial. As journalists, we hope the P.S. will describe or explain the issue we've raised. That's interviewing by accident. If you get somebody who doesn't want to play, you're in trouble."

Most of the time, in friendly interviews, the source adds the P.S. "out of charity. Because our social instincts tell us to be nice. Their charity—not the question—delivers the answer. We're relying on them to help us out. Relying on people's charity to get answers is not a good practice. The ones we need charity from the most are the least likely to give it—the people who stand to lose something." And certain people rarely give charity: "People who go by the book—cops, bureaucrats, lawyers—people who take questions literally, people who are nervous. The last thing fearful people do is open up. They shut down." Professional answer givers, what Sawatsky calls sophisticated politicians and business executives, frequently defeat journalists by answering a closed-ended question with a curt "No, not at all" or a disingenuous "Gosh, I hope not!" before switching to a prepackaged "message track," the spiel they had planned to use to answer any uncomfortable questions.

Sawatsky has compiled a list he calls the "Seven Deadly Sins" or what to avoid in an interview. In subsequent chapters, we'll explain in detail the strategies you'll need to use to make every interview successful.

1. **Failing to ask a question.** If you're making a statement, you're not asking a question. Your job is to get informa-

tion from sources, not to impress them with your superior knowledge. When reporters make statements, they allow sources to avoid answering questions.

2. **Asking two questions at once, also known as asking "double barrel" questions.** Example of a double barrel question: "Who did you like interviewing least and what's your most impressive interviewing coup?" Sources will naturally gravitate to answering questions that make them look best and avoid those whose answers might be less than flattering to their reputations.

3. **Overloading questions.** By putting too much information into a question, the source with something to hide can easily keep it hidden. For example, when reporters were trying to find out if President Bill Clinton had had a long-standing affair with a woman named Gennifer Flowers, a well-known television reporter misused his opportunity by asking an overloaded question.

> **Reporter:** "Was Gennifer Flowers your lover for 12 years?"
> **Clinton:** "That allegation is false."

Which allegation is false? That she was his lover? Or that she was his lover for 12 years? Maybe she was his lover for 11 years or seven years, in which case, Clinton answered truthfully. By asking imprecise questions, reporters allow sources to wriggle out of responding to issues that are difficult for them.

4. **Adding statements or comments to questions.** Even adding an innocuous statement can derail a good question. Instead of answering the question, the source

answers the comment. A good example of a lost opportunity can be seen in an interview with former American hostage Terry Anderson. Anderson, who spent seven years as a hostage in Lebanon, shared his prison cell with other hostages. After he was released, Anderson did dozens of interviews, answering questions about what his life as a hostage had been like. During one television interview, the reporter asked him:

"What would go through your mind in the quiet times? Because there must have been times when you didn't talk to each other."
Anderson: "Oh sure there were times when we didn't talk to each other; we had to get out of that room by getting out of our minds."

Instead of answering the excellent question—"What went through your mind?"—Anderson answered the comment: "There must have been times when you didn't talk to each other."

The interviewer's statement is about as benign as they come, which is precisely Sawatsky's point. The content of the statement doesn't matter. Most people will respond to the last phrase out of the interviewer's mouth. As a consequence, we never learn what went through Anderson's mind. We miss an opportunity to find out first hand what hostages think about when being held in captivity for seven years. By interjecting statements, "we lose our ability to get precise comments," Sawatsky explains.

5. **Using loaded or "trigger" words in questions.** Some words are obviously loaded. Let's say a local university's

president has proposed replacing the English department with a school of journalism. You've been assigned the story. You begin the interview by asking: "How will you sell this scheme to the board of trustees?" More than likely, the president will respond by attacking your use of the word scheme; he will respond not to the question, but to the trigger word: "This is not a scheme. This is a well-thought-out plan . . ." By using the word "scheme," you've allowed the president to ignore an important question—How will he convince the board of trustees to go along with the plan? Moreover, it gives the president a forum—free publicity really—to sell an uncritical version of his controversial plan to your readers or viewers.

6. **Using hyperbole, or asking hyperbolic questions.** When reporters ask sources hyperbolic questions— "What does it feel like to be a sex God?" "What does it feel like to be a superstar?" "What does it feel like to be a hero?"—we can predict the response will almost always be modest. Sources tend to want to counterbalance hyperbolic questions with humble responses. Instead of using generalizations, ask your sources to answer specific questions focusing on evidence that suggest they're a sex God, a superstar, or a hero.

7. **Asking closed-ended questions.** Sources with something to hide, or a message to get across, will usually answer a closed-ended question with a curt "No, not at all," "Gosh, I hope not!" or "Sure, but. . ." followed by their prepared message or defense. Several years ago, an owner of a major league baseball team had made statements that led to accusations that she was a racist. When

she appeared on a network news show, she was asked "Are you a racist?" The answer was predictable. She said: "No, not at all," and proceeded to offer for the network's viewers the message she wanted them to hear. "Of course she's going to deny," says Sawatsky. The reporters "are trying by magic to confront her, hoping she'll reveal something of herself. Once she denies that she's a racist, where does that leave the reporter?"

Instead, ask questions that begin with what, why, and how, followed by who, when, and where. Present sources with particular allegations of racism, child abuse, or swindling and ask open ended questions that force them to respond to incidents rather than generalities.

Sidebar 3.2: Tales from the Street

Veteran reporter and editor Matt Coker recalls one of his most impressive interviewing mishaps:

> I don't remember if we were still called "cub reporters" back when I first started my career with a daily newspaper, but I was very young when I found out that the chief of staff for California's then-Lt. Governor Leo McCarthy lived within our circulation area, which was eastern L.A. County/western San Bernardino County. McCarthy had an office in the state building in downtown L.A., so I arranged to interview the chief of staff for a profile there. For some reason, I had experienced several nightmares when venturing into downtown L.A. as a reporter. This was probably the most embarrassing. I got all decked out for the interview—slacks, wool sportscoat, Italian silk shirt and tie. I think by then I was already disillusioned with the mainstream press and—in the back of my mind—I was

angling for a future PR job with McCarthy. "Why look at this well-dressed young man," the chief of staff would say. "He belongs on our team."

So, like I said, I'm all dressed up. My long hair—that was the style then—was perfect. Unfortunately, it was one of the hottest days of the year and my little car had no air conditioning. To make sure my hair stayed put, I kept the windows rolled up. And, for some stupid reason, I also kept my wool coat on for the bumper-to-bumper ride to Los Angeles.

I finally got downtown, and this denizen of the sticks soon discovered one of the mysteries of urban life: it costs money to park your car. I didn't have any money. For one thing, I was poor. For another, what little money I did have my wife didn't trust me to carry. I drove around for blocks and blocks—hot day, windows rolled up, wool coat on—and couldn't find a free parking space. Finally, noticing I was going to be late to my interview, I parked in the state building parking structure. I took the ticket from the machine, sprinted into the building. By the time I arrived, I was dripping with sweat from the heat and nervousness.

Riding the elevator up to McCarthy's office, I could see in the reflection from the metal doors that my Italian silk suit was drenched in sweat around my armpits. I buttoned my coat to cover it up. Nice save! Couldn't do much about the long hair stuck to my wet neck and face, though.

I interviewed the chief of staff, a heck of a nice guy who for some unknown reason urged me to read Paul Theroux's *The Mosquito Coast.* Perhaps noticing my wet hair and face and the pool of sweat forming under my chair, he also urged me to take off my coat. I did. By now, my Italian silk shirt was clinging to me like I was made of glue. It was at this point the chief of staff asked me the question that I had hoped he wouldn't: "Would you like to meet the lieutenant governor?"

Um, okay.

We walked into McCarthy's office. He had his coat off, too, but his shirt was drier than the Sahara. And his hair—unlike mine—was perfect. "Nice to meet you, Matt," said the second-most-powerful-man in the state. "A little hot out there?"

Needless to say, I wasn't offered the PR job.

It wasn't until I got to my car that I realized I had no way of leaving the parking structure without paying. I walked around downtown for awhile. I looked around on the ground for spare change. Finally, I boldly decided it was time to take matters into my own hands. I called my wife and asked her to please come and bring me some money. About an hour later she arrived with the seven bucks that would liberate my car. I drove home—with every window in the car rolled down and that damn wool coat in the trunk!

may not be difficult. They know the police and fire chiefs, high-level cops, and perhaps some paramedics. These journalists also have a leg up in gathering information because the officials are more apt to talk to them on the basis of past contacts.

The green or just-hired reporter has a tougher job but a doable one. Usually, any law enforcement person or firefighter can point out a chief or the ranking officer at the scene. As for witnesses and survivors, approach them on the spot. Shyness or hesitancy are not a good fit for journalism—especially when time is crucial. Simply introduce yourself, show your press card, and begin asking questions. Bear in mind, however, that these are individuals under stress and are not trained observers. Keep your voice level and your queries brief. In the case of police, firefighters and paramedics, don't attempt to shoot questions while they are hauling out the wounded or directing an operation. Wait for the moment when they are free and then go to them. You may not have long so make your time count. Still, brevity doesn't mean that you can't ask follow-up questions. Is an investigation under way? Could the blast have been caused by a bomb? If so, is there a possibility of a terrorist element? Was it a gas explosion? If so, had the tenants smelled gas before the structure blew up? Was the gas company called? Who called? How did the survivors get out? What's the dollar value of the damage? Probe also for feature elements: oddball happenings, unusual valor, a miraculous survival.

A careful approach might be necessary for survivors, who may be suffering from shock. Empathy counts here. Try to convey the idea that you understand what they've been through. If their account lacks continuity or complete coherence, go over the missing facts slowly and patiently until the picture becomes complete—or at least as complete as you can get it. Often, a reporter must interview two, three, or four survivors to pull together a full and true account. With survivors, attempt to plumb their personal experience in the tragedy. Seek details on how they got through the ordeal. Did they save anyone or were they themselves saved? By whom? Do they know what caused the explosion? Get their personal reaction to the calamity. Take notes or get it on tape.

There are times in such situations when obtaining information becomes much easier than you feared. Some people need little prompting to unload their stories. It may be a form of catharsis. *Los Angeles Times* foreign correspondent John Daniszewski experienced this while covering the hordes of refugees streaming out of Kosovo into Albania during the NATO bombing of the province in 1999.

Writing about the assignment in the International Press Institute's magazine *Report,* Daniszewski recalled that the fleeing victims ". . . often found in the correspondents at the border the first sympathetic ear upon which to pour their wrenching tales of killings, arson, robberies and other cruelties." One man, before he was even questioned by the reporter, cried out, "Five of my sons have been killed." He then, without prompting, went on to describe the massacre of 50 to 70 young men by a river.

Witnesses, who are victims, also require your attention. Eyewitness accounts are best. Try to track down original sources when you get second- or third-hand information from faces in the crowd. Occasionally, the task becomes easy. Eyewitnesses seek out reporters to pour out what they have seen or heard. When the Air France Concorde crashed near Paris on July 25, 2000, with the loss of 113 lives, several people who watched in horror as the plane went down gave the media graphic descriptions of the disaster. Witnesses included survivors at the hotel the Concorde slammed into.

Such outpourings are not uncommon in covering breaking news. Take full advantage of such opportunities but don't count on getting them easily. There will be many times when you have to draw people out by evincing understanding of their situation. Some journalists, in an ongoing story, have won the confidence of sources by living with them, sharing their trials. An example was Ernie Pyle, the great World War II correspondent who literally became one with the GIs he was writing about, lying in their foxholes, eating their chow, and putting his life in jeopardy every day. He was with a combat unit when he was killed by a sniper in the South Pacific. For months before his death he had filed dispatches with an insight and warmth unmatched in war reporting. Soldiers knew they could talk to Pyle freely, even complain about their officers, knowing that he would never violate their trust.

More recently, a similar approach was used by *Newsweek* photographer Robert King, who spent several days with Chechen rebels as Russian forces were attacking them in late 1999. Not only was King able to shoot vivid pictures, he also gained material for an exclusive, first-person article for his magazine that included interviews with a rebel commander and his men. King, who wrote, "I'm doing my best to blend in with my companions," was provided with personal bodyguards, shown devastated towns and villages, and eventually gotten safely out of Chechnya, a breakaway Russian province. Of course, the rebels were no fools. They realized the propaganda value to their cause of having an American reporter tell their story to the world. But so what? That fact didn't concern King. He objectively reported what he saw and heard, leaving the reader to form his or her own opinion of the conflict. That's called good journalism.

Interviewing at the Courts and City Hall

Journalists should anticipate impromptu interviews at venues other than the scenes of disasters such as earthquakes, shootings, plane crashes, fires, and explosions. Events can happen fast at the courts, city hall, even the school board. Public meetings and court sessions are programmed, but a lot of information gathering for reporters takes place before and after meetings, during breaks in the proceedings, in courthouse corridors, and outside the buildings. Scores of interviews occur on courthouse steps as prosecutors and defense lawyers emerge from a courtroom.

Let's first examine your moves at, say, a city council meeting. Get there early, particularly if you are weak on agenda items. That's the time to buttonhole the city manager, clerk, and individual council members. Most likely, copies of the agenda will be made available to the public before the meeting so you can scan it and prepare your questions. There isn't much time so make your queries brief, asking for an explanation of the fuzziest issues to enable you to follow the discussion. If a recess is declared, continue your interviewing, probably with more assurance

because you now know more. If you haven't satisfied yourself by the end of the meeting, stick around. The officials
will have more time to talk to you, an exercise that benefits
them as much as you and your readers or viewers. Ask clear,
to-the-point questions followed by additional questions if
the answers are muddy. The idea is to meet your deadline
fully prepared to write or broadcast a coherent story. Even
if sources are interviewed live, a television or radio reporter
often must provide further explanation and background
for their audiences. If there is time following a meeting,
you might suggest a nearby coffee shop for an interview.
It's a relaxing venue that could loosen up a stuffy official.

A similar approach works at the courthouse. The difference is that the atmosphere is more formal and restricted.
Some judges in high profile trials won't even permit interviews in the corridor outside the courtroom much less
inside. An example was the famed O. J. Simpson murder
trial a few years ago when the judge issued strict instructions
against such encounters. This is rare, however, and
reporters usually can confer with attorneys and witnesses
during a recess and before and after a day's session. Interviews and news conferences on the courthouse steps happen
often. Before the start of a trial, prosecutors and defense
lawyers may comment on their strategies and name the witnesses they plan to call. A defendant in a criminal trial also
might be willing to talk to the media if he is free on bail.
Reporters face a tougher challenge if the person is behind
bars, although not an impossible one. Jailhouse interviews
are not uncommon and have led to front-page stories. They
also may lead to an involuntary court appearance by the
reporter as we shall see later.

One trial figure, a juror, is absolutely off limits as an interview source. If a judge discovered such a violation of court rules he would dismiss the juror and perhaps declare a mistrial. However, a member of the jury or an alternate juror who has been discharged for medical reasons or a violation of court instructions is fair game. In some cases, these individuals have given their opinion of lawyers' tactics, the evidence, and have suggested what verdict they would have rendered if they had remained on the jury. Obviously such disclosures irritate judges, sometimes to the point where they cite a reporter and/or a newspaper for contempt if the interview is published. The results of an ex-juror interview can lead to a discussion between the reporter, her supervisor, and the news organization's lawyer on what can be printed or broadcast. Responsible newspapers, magazines, and broadcasters do not want to be the cause of a mistrial. At the same time, they do not want to pass up what could be an exclusive story. Post-trial interviews with jurors are generally within legal bounds, but a particular judge may decide to put them off limits by instructing the panelists to shun the press.

A safer source for comment on a criminal or civil trial are attorneys and other experts who have no connection with the proceedings. They are free to opine on prosecution and defense strategies, the impact of the testimony of a particular witness, or the makeup of the jury. A famous criminal lawyer, for instance, can provide an educated view of how a felony trial is going for one side or the other. Some reporters have a "usual suspects" list of prominent trial attorneys they can call on for their take on a major trial. Most likely they will not offer observations on the guilt or innocence of a defendant, nor should the question be asked—at least not for the record. The Simpson criminal trial spawned at least a dozen pundits on radio and television who regularly aired their views on the proceeding.

On the other hand, relatives of the defendant(s) and victims can provide good copy or air time. In most instances, they are accessible for interviews (often hurriedly on the courthouse steps), the former because they want to proclaim the innocence of the accused and the latter because they want punishment meted out. The suspect's kin may also relay his or her reaction to jail conditions if he is incarcerated. Be very careful in these talks not to suggest or even hint of a bias for one party or the other. The unwanted result of such a lapse in judgment is that the individual may expect your story to be tilted in the suspect's or the victim's favor. Of course, the facts of some news accounts are weighed so heavily against a defendant that the reader or viewer is likely to feel repugnance toward him. That's not your responsibility as long as you have written or broadcast a fair and balanced report. When three young people were charged with fatally beating a gay college student in Wyoming the evidence was so overwhelming that undoubtedly the general public was revolted by the crime. Yet, newswriters took special pains to give a straight account. You must keep in mind that the law calls for a presumption of innocence, no matter how heinous the crime. How journalists are hindered by judicial gag orders will be discussed in a later chapter.

Even under the severest strain and heartbreak, many people will willingly talk to reporters who display a degree of sensitivity. A California physician, whose wife was accused of the shooting death of three of their children, permitted a full interview with the *Los Angeles Times*. He described the victims as good students despite the fact that two of them had to overcome physical difficulties. The father, crying at times, also revealed that he would never live in the family home again. It was a moving feature and not easy to obtain. Reporter Caitlin Liu said she "laid the groundwork" by sending the doctor a handwritten note requesting the interview and also tried to convince his employees that he should grant it.

These proved to be good moves, Liu recalled. "For one thing," she explained, "he liked our first story of the deaths because of its accuracy. I learned later from his brother that he selected my note from several other requests for interviews because it was gentle and not intrusive. Other reporters, he went on, wrote demanding notes that were abrasive in their approach."

Their meeting, Liu remembers, "was a little intimidating at first" since the physician had brought along his brother and several officers from the sheriff's department, who instructed him not to discuss the day of the murders or the progress of the investigation. "These were ground rules I could live with," Liu went on. She started off with prepared questions, gradually getting to the heart of the story. "I thought a lot about the questions I would ask and believe the interview went great," she remarked. Liu further noted that she began the interview with "casual small talk. I didn't even turn on my tape recorder for the first few minutes." This is a technique used by most professional journalists, who warm up the subject before settling down for the important dialogue.

A chilling example of a complaint interviewee occurred in San Francisco, where a man hacked his girlfriend to death with an axe. As police were leading him out of his apartment in handcuffs, he turned to reporters and said. "Boys, I have one of the best butchers in town and there are two fine steaks in the fridge that you can have." There were no takers.

Sue Russell, an internationally syndicated journalist, stressed "tact and sympathy as great tools" for an interview. "They are also crucial when interviewing any kind of victims, particularly family members," she avers. Russell, who writes for top-level newspapers and magazines here and abroad, says her approach is to "acknowledge their suffering over losing a loved one and I also acknowledge that that it was all being made additionally painful by the media coverage. If someone senses that you are seeing things from their perspective and are sensitive to their situation, often that's all it takes to get them to open up."

Political Interviews

Covering politics is often anything but static. Just as in covering crime and disasters, the reporter must be ready to think quickly and creatively when reporting on various aspects of the political process. An example is a speech by a candidate for a major office. You will likely get an advance text of the address, which you can follow along as the speaker holds forth. An easy task? Not always. For one thing, the candidate may deviate from the script—or dump it altogether—tossing in unexpected comments, new accusations against his opponent, or an admission of some youthful indiscretion that has been rumored: "I think I may have inhaled once or twice." The reporter also must note audience reaction to certain parts of the address.

Last-minute changes in a prepared speech often mean a quick trip to the podium to ask the speaker the reason for the switch and to perhaps expand upon his new thoughts. And even if he stuck to the text 100 percent, there may be a need for him to explain some elements of the talk so you can write a story that makes sense to readers and not leave them wondering about what was left out. There is also the possibility that you might have to interview others— election rivals he may have attacked in the talk or maybe a political guru or other politicians for their opinion of it. These chores often must be done quickly, requiring the reporter to have direct questions in mind before picking up the phone. If the respondent has not heard the talk, you have to quickly summarize it for him and possibly read him part of it. Hope that he will accept your summary for comment purposes.

Riding the campaign trail requires even more nimble footedness. Candidates are likely to deliver recycled stump speeches at each stop. They may be new to local audiences but not to distant readers or viewers who may have seen stories about the same address given three days earlier at another location. To stay on top of the story, the reporter must explore other news possibilities. This may involve seeking an impromptu interview with the candidate or talking to her staff members, even if it's on a not-for-attribution basis, meaning you cannot link the source to the information. Or it could take the form of searching out local residents for their impression of the candidate of the moment or their thoughts about an opponent, who preceded her in addressing the community. Local or regional party officials also are prime targets for determining the political mood of the populace. Hordes of journalists followed both the Republican and Democratic presidential aspirants on the 2000 campaign trail. The reporting proved to be a mere warm-up for the wild and unprecedented Florida vote-count dispute after election day. Print and broadcast reporters interviewed everybody in sight while their home-office counterparts were trolled for comments about the imbroglio in their areas and overseas. Never were so many politicians, lawyers, state officials, election workers, or bystanders interviewed by so many media people. The better interviewers stood out because they asked incisive questions that went to the bone of the issue. They followed one question with another when they believed the answer was fuzzy or simply self-serving. If you watched the action on television, you probably noticed that a subject would frequently end the interview when he or she thought the queries were hitting too close to the truth. Only in the abstract do many public figures share the journalist's aim for the truth. In Florida, spin, which we shall discuss in detail later, dominated the scene.

In the voting mess, a solid knowledge of the issue was vital for a newsworthy interview. In a tight deadline atmosphere, there is little time for small talk. Questions should be short, to the point, and sometimes provocative. Some interviews will take place in press conference formats where you are vying with your colleagues for the subject's attention. But strive to get away from the herd for exclusive interviews with candidates and others. This may depend on how well the individual knows and trusts you. Still, don't be afraid of approaching someone cold or trying to arrange a meeting through her press secretary or other associate. Reporting calls for bold action. Think of waking up the next morning to read that a rival has grabbed the interview you only thought about getting.

Although speed is important in today's highly competitive market, it should not take precedence over fairness and accuracy. If you can snatch a scoop, fine, but be sure that doubtful statements from an interviewee are accompanied by contrary information garnered from your own knowledge or from other sources. The late James "Scotty" Reston, a top Washington reporter and columnist for *The New York Times,* once wrote: ". . . gather your own information about people as much as you can; test every popular conception; and don't be in a hurry about people."

Bernard Kalb, moderator of CNN's "Reliable Sources." put it this way: "A journalist's job is to penetrate the fog, smog, and gibberish that's heaped on the press by various sources and see if you can extract the basic news."

Often, the closer to the end of an election, the dirtier it gets. In the final days of Los Angeles' mayoral race in 2001, negative ads began sprouting on radio and via unsourced phone calls to voters. One aspirant was accused of helping a drug dealer get out of prison, another was the victim of an anti-semitic attack and so on. It was virtually impossible to trace the ads (the candidates, of course, denied responsibility), but Los Angeles Times reporters James Rainey and Massie Ritsch interviewed the incumbent mayor and religious and community leaders, who roundly condemned the hate messages. This was quick-thinking journalism. It might have taken weeks to find the providers of the ads. By its action, the Times gave readers something to think about before they entered the voting booth.

Sports and Business Interviews

The world of sports has been overtaken by the real world of big money, corruption, and politics. The game is still paramount but its coverage is only one facet of the reporter's job. Writers must deal with cities competing for Major League teams in football, basketball, and baseball. Colleges are under close scrutiny by the National Collegiate Athletic Association for rules violations. Trades involving players making millions of dollars are on Page 1 of sports sections and may lead off sports segment broadcasts. At this moment, an NBA player is charged with murder; a Major League infielder is the center of an investigation over his being signed by a club although he was underage; and more than one college is in trouble for recruiting missteps. And it's highly likely that similar problems are occurring as you read this.

All this means that today's sportswriter must be knowledgeable about more than athletic rules and how to interpret league trades. He or she should have some understanding of the business side of sports, an investigative bent to uncover illegalities, and sociological and educational aspects of college competition. More sports reporters are examining such issues as how many college athletes graduate, the courses they take, how they are recruited, and the growing rate of criminal charges against players. A Los Angeles radio station features "The athlete arrest of the week" in its sports broadcast. Questions may have to be asked not only of athletes but academic officials, school athletic directors, and parents of players. Often these queries are be timed to meet deadlines so reporters must have sufficient background to obtain answers quickly and understandably. In the past, the sports section was considered the lighter side of the newspaper—sometimes derisively as the "toy department"—and reporters' questions were frequently gentle. This still happens, but a growing number of sportswriters and columnists are digging hard for hard news and their stories reflect it. In some cases, reporters have been kicked out of locker rooms and shunned by coaches for asking the tough questions. This is in sharp contrast to banal, newsless queries that produce such responses as: "This is a big one and we gotta win the big ones," or "I think I got more confidence in myself than in my last fight."

In its *Guide for Sports Reporters,* Investigative Reporters & Editors (IRE), a national organization based at the University of Missouri's School of Journalism, tenders this advice in interviewing sports figures on controversial situations: "Listen for clues as to what they are really saying. Don't give them a chance to back out by asking, 'Do you have a couple of minutes to talk?' Start right in asking questions. If time permits, ask them about themselves and their families. . . Listen to answers. Do they respond to what you asked? Paraphrase the answer back to see if the source concurs that is exactly what he or she meant."

IRE also recommends that the reporter tell the source everything that will be printed. "Don't surprise them. Make it clear what damage their quotes can do."

Interviewing comes easiest to reporters who have a thorough knowledge of the game they are covering. College journalism majors with an eye toward future professional sports writing often start by reporting games on their own campuses for the student newspaper. On bigger papers they will learn that the trend is toward incisive, in-depth writing with a strong emphasis on human interest. Effective interviewing often means getting beyond the stock impression of athletes and coaches to look at them as mere mortals with hang-ups, fears, and ideas—sometimes unexpected ones—about the systems of which they are a part. Doug Flutie, a quarterback for the Buffalo Bills, expressed his feelings to *Los Angeles Times* reporter T. J. Simmers when another quarterback was picked by the team coach to start a crucial playoff game. "The thing that frustrates me more than anything is that I've been waiting 10 years for this opportunity," Flutie said. Commented Simmers: "This is business more than sport, and although that makes mockery of all that coaching tripe about team chemistry, loyalty . . . (coach Wade) Phillips has already earned his pay. Hired to determine the best course to win, he believes the No. 1 defense in the league needs a boost from the offense to survive the tortuous road ahead."

Take Notes, Evaluate Them Later

In covering a story on the run, a notebook or tape recorder should always be in your hand. Sponge-like, absorb almost everything, even though you know you will not use it all. The point is to collect all the information you can so you have the luxury of tossing out later what you won't need. There usually is little or no time to fully evaluate what you are recording; that will come when you are writing the story. Jim Stasiowski, a writing coach for various newspapers, offers this advice in the New Mexico Press Association newsletter to reporters ready to compose their piece: "Leave out anything marginal: The great quotation isn't great if it doesn't fit precisely the story you're working on. I don't care if the mayor told you a very meaningful anecdote about Philippine monkeys, it will not fit the story about repairs to the sewage-treatment plant."

5

Breaking Down the Barriers

Elsa Walsh, a writer for *The New Yorker* magazine, was interviewing Tipper Gore, wife of the then-vice-president, Albert Gore. The interview was not going well. Mrs. Gore, never one to seek publicity, was guarded, especially in response to questions about reported criticisms of her husband's presidential campaign at the time. When her questions drew only tepid responses, Walsh decided to take a different direction. She mentioned that she had been told that once a week in the mid-1990s, Mrs. Gore had traveled with a medical van that provided services to the mentally ill.

"For the next forty-five minutes, she was transformed," Walsh wrote. "She told stories. She recounted how she had chased a homeless man named Jack down a crowded street, with Secret Service agents in pursuit, how he was nearly naked and she was in jogging clothes . . ."

From that point, the interview swung into high gear and Walsh drew out enough material for an engaging *New Yorker* profile.

The reporter was merely employing a tactic that many experienced journalists rely on when an interview seems to be stalled because of barriers thrown up by the subject:

switch to a more comfortable topic to put the other at ease. Reporters dread leaving empty-handed. It's a matter of professional pride and the fact that their editors are waiting for a publishable story. The reporter must use any ethical means to crack the wall set up by reluctant, shy, hostile, or tongue-tied subjects.

Associated Press Special Correspondent Linda Deutsch, who has interviewed dozens of celebrities, counsels: "Don't be afraid to express admiration for the subject, if you really do admire him or her." She cites an interview with Pulitzer Prize-winning playwright William Inge that was foundering. "He was very shy and had been giving me yes or no answers, which is a nightmare for a journalist," Deutsch says. "So, at one point, I told him I cried whenever I saw his play 'Come Back, Little Sheba.' He said he cries, too, when he sees it on stage and he broke into tears right then. This broke the ice. You must connect with the person. If necessary, tell him something about yourself. Being cool and distant is not the right approach for an interview."

At the same time, avoid fawning over the source, no matter how big a celebrity. This can lead to mushy, worshipful copy. In a *Los Angeles Times* article on the superficiality of some TV interviews, Mimi Avins wrote: "Celebrity worship hangs on the belief that Hollywood's best are gods and goddesses who live in harmony on Mt. Olympus (or Malibu). They're all wonderful people blessed with kind souls and natural charms . . ."

The writer might draw on his or her own background to pry open the subject, coming up with an incident or recollection that touches a nerve. *Los Angeles Times'* sports staffer Mike DiGiovanna was interviewing former Boston

Red Sox catcher Carlton Fisk but was getting nowhere with the tight-lipped New Englander. "He wouldn't give much more than one-word or one-sentence answers to my questions," wrote DiGiovanna in the *Times*. But the reporter got an idea. He told Fisk that when he was in junior high school in East Lyme, Connecticut, he and his classmates would get into fistfights over who was better, Fisk or ex-New York Yankee catcher Thurman Munson.

The recollection transformed the interview. "A twinkle came into Fisk's eye," DiGiovanna related. "His whole body perked up. It was as if someone had pumped a 10-cappuccino IV through his veins and released his vocal chords . . . The rest of the interview was a breeze."

If you use this tactic be sure you call up the right memory, something to which the person can relate. A closed-mouthed labor chieftain, for instance, might open up if you mentioned that your father had been a union member or that you had just read a book about the early struggles of organized labor to gain acceptance, assuming, of course, he was and you did.

Sometimes a simple comment about a family photo or other object on the individual's desk can trigger a response. It's also okay to admire her dress, hair-do or jewelry, marvel at his coffee-cup collection, or wonder aloud about her ability to arrive at the office at six in the morning and plunge into work. In short, do what it takes to get the interview moving. If five or ten minutes of small talk is needed, give up the time. If the source wants your tape recorder turned off, don't argue about it. Remember, you are the seeker and he is the giver. In essence, you are there by permission. "The key to successful interviewing is to get people to open up without giving them the impression that you are prying or interrogating, though you may be doing just that," counsels Cindy Yorks, a Southern California-based freelancer. Yorks, who writes for *Harper's Bazaar, People, Women's Day,* the *Los Angeles Times* and other publications, adds: "Word your questions so the subject can't get away with a yes or no. Give them opportunities to expand their answers by following up with other questions."

This, according to Yorks, saves the reporter's time and possibly eliminates the need for follow-up calls—especially important when time is a crucial factor. In her experience, Yorks says, "Some subjects like to open up. Others try to steer the interview in another direction. Stay focused and press them for answers you need. When wrapping up an interview, I like to ask the subject to add anything he or she cares to that I have not covered." The closing question apparently nettled French movie star Catherine Deneuve during Yorks' interview with her while riding in a limousine, the writer remembers. "When I asked if she had anything to add, she sighed, looked out the window and said, 'I knew the ride would be too long.'"

Another California writer, Arline Inge, who specializes in food and world travel, declares that her first step in an interview "is to establish rapport. I start out with small talk to search out common ground. Once that's established, I try to involve the subject in my project. For example, I might say, 'Our readers are really interested in the fact that you are a successful working mother.'"

Inge also ends an interview by asking the source if there is something he or she wants to say that was not covered. "And I offer to telephone them a few days later after we both have had time to think of follow-up questions. I give them my own phone number as well."

Why Won't He Talk?

Reasons vary as to why some interviews are harder than others. For a number of people, meeting the press is a new and perhaps frightening experience. They also may harbor negative feelings toward the media based on what they've read or seen in the movies. They or someone they know also may have had a bad encounter with a reporter, newspaper, or TV crew. Then there is the individual who's in trouble— under indictment, in bankruptcy, politically embarrassed, or is a fallen hero. Others are basically not outgoing people and have trouble communicating with anyone, much less a reporter. Or they may just be naturally shy. Eric Nalder, a Pulitzer Prize-winning investigative reporter, and a member of Investigative Reporters & Editors (IRE), says his technique in dealing with "no comment" sources is simple. "I tell them not to worry, that it's no big deal, that he is just one of several people I've talked to. Then I say, 'Here's what I know about the situation. Let's talk about this part a little bit.' Then I start talking about the information I want to confirm," he said on an IRE panel.

When someone says he is afraid to comment, Nalder responds "with a little sympathy and a lot of reassurance," telling him he understands his concern. "Give glancing recognition to their concerns, but try to move right on to the point of the story," the newsman urges. Nalder also believes "it doesn't hurt to say you need the person's help."

"Who is going to explain this to me if you don't?" might be a way to put it, he offers.

Whatever reason for the barrier, it must be cracked. When opposition is indicated you should proceed cautiously. If, for example, the subject is a teacher who has been suspended for alleged child molestation, don't open the interview with, "Did you do it?" That could kill the interview on the spot. Leave such direct interrogation to the police. (If, however, he volunteers to admit or deny his guilt, it could be the lead of your story.) First, win that person's confidence. Put him at ease with innocuous questions, such as how many years he has taught, his previous employment, honors he may have won, or where he grew up. Then gradually get to the purpose of the meeting, which is to get a news or feature story. At some point, you must get to the heart of the charges against him and persuade him to tell his side. John Fried, a former reporter for the *Wall Street Journal* and other publications, once told a journalism class: "If you start out with a sensitive question, the interview could be over in thirty seconds."

Expressing empathy with shy or reluctant interviewees is a valuable tool. "Not a transparent veneer of empathy but the real thing," insists Sue Russell, a Los Angeles-based, internationally syndicated journalist and book author. "I try to put myself inside my interview subjects' heads. If they feel misunderstood, I want them immediately to sense that this experience will be different. There are occasions when it's useful to anger a subject or put them on the defensive, but this is not one of them. When there are tough but vital questions hovering over an interview, I always frame them silently first to try to eliminate the risk of inadvertently closing the emotional door between us."

Russell recounts she once interviewed a notoriously prickly public figure who had just filed for bankruptcy. Worried that he might become irritable and cut her off, she noted that he had filed Chapter 11 not Chapter 7. "Perhaps he felt there was some honor in repaying some of his debts," Russell explains. "I decided to ease in by asking how important it was for him to be able to do that. Not only did it not terminate the interview but afterwards he expressed surprise at his own candor. He said, 'Boy if anyone else had asked me some of the things you just asked me, I would have ended it.' That's it really. Tread softly and carry a big stick."

Another journalist who fine-tunes his interviews on sensitive topics is Eric Newhouse, who won a Pulitzer Prize in 2000 for his 12-month series on the economic and social costs of alcoholism. The veteran reporter for the *Great Falls* (Montana) *Tribune* explains: "Interviewing is less a technique than it is a frame of mind. To me, interviewing means giving people the opportunity to tell their stories in the best way they can. My job is to define an issue, find the best people to illustrate different aspects of it, and then encourage them to talk about these issues."

To accomplish that goal in the series, Newhouse had to steer a careful course with people laboring under stress and shame.

He developed what he calls a "three-fold strategy" that got people to talk. "No one wanted to discuss his or her dirty laundry on the record," he comments, "so first I emphasized that alcoholism is a medical disease, not a moral failing, so there need be no stigma to being ill. Second, I talked about what good this series could do about educating the public about a serious problem. Third, I told them the stories would have no impact—and the newspaper no credibility—without using full names and pictures of the victims."

Most of the subjects agreed to the interviews, facing the issue squarely and allowing their names and photos to be used, including a woman who had been date-raped while drunk, and members of two families, who had coped with an alcoholic parent. When the newspaper celebrated Newhouse's Pulitzer, journalism's highest honor, in its offices, six of his interviewees showed up to offer their congratulations. Said one about his initial request to question her: "My first thought was 'Oh my God,' but you put me and my family at ease right from the start. You do have a way with people."

Approaching withdrawn individuals often depends on the person and the circumstance. *New Yorker* staff writer Joan Acocella says she has found that "shyness is almost always in response to questions about their personal lives, and what I do at that point is just back off and ask them about their work, which they are usually glad to discuss." On the other hand, some persons, although initially shy, may loosen up, even about their personal lives, especially when it's in their interest. Such a result may take a little more time but patience is in an interviewer's favor.

Always remember that different situations may call for different paths to a fulfilling interview. The factors could include the subject himself, the nature or sensitivity of the subject, the place and time of the meeting, or others who may be present. Some top executives or entertainment celebrities want their public relations aides to sit in. Don't object. It's their prerogative. In the case of a whistle-blower, it's best to call him or her at their home, not at their place of business.

Shirley Camper Soman, a New York-based veteran book and magazine author, recalls that when she was preparing a book involving oral history, "I deliberately did not find out anything about the subjects before interviewing them. I went in cold. I would say, 'Please tell me about yourself because I don't know anything about you.' This was very productive. People like to talk about themselves, especially older people." Soman, whose specializations include health, aging, and social issues, notes, however, that on other assignments she starts out with questions. "I try my best to find out what their interests are, what they like and don't like, and what they think. If they hold back and are worried about what they say, I assure them that whatever they don't want in print will be thrown out. But I also tell them that what they say may be important to other people."

Dan Hurley interviewed about 25,000 people on the streets of Chicago for his book, *The 60-Second Novelist: What 22,613 People Taught Me About Life*. After each interview, Hurley would hand the passer-by a free, one-page story of his or her life based on their chat. From this, he became convinced that a reporter can ask someone about almost anything if he or she loses their misgivings or timidity. "The reason we like Oprah and Barbara Walters is that they ask the questions we're afraid to ask," he points out. "These are the questions we must ask because the journalist has a special role. We are the designated askers."

Hurley, who has written other books and articles for a number of leading magazines, including *McCall's, Reader's Digest* and *Good Housekeeping,* insists an interview often produces the best results when the questions are sharp, incisive, and even embarrassing. "Some questions should make you tingle a bit when you ask them," he says. "If you are not putting out questions that make you a little nervous, you are probably not asking very interesting questions. An interview is not a normal social situation. Don't squander your opportunity."

According to Hurley, a smile helps when you are posing a question such as, "Didn't you feel like a bastard when you left your wife and children and ran off with your secretary?"

"Don't worry about his reaction," insists Hurley. "He knows that everybody wants to know this and he's probably been asked the same question by his family and friends."

Hurley is absolutely correct when he advocates a bald, fearless interview style. Just keep in mind that the hard-hitting queries should come after a few softer, warm-up questions. A pitcher doesn't throw his fast ball before loosening up in the bullpen.

Parade magazine Senior Editor Fran Carpentier, who passes judgment on a lot of freelance submissions, insists that, "Every word in an interview must be pure gold. Saying something is 'fabulous' won't do. A simple affirmation does not work for us. The interview must contain something revealing or that smacks of the subject's personality. I want fresh quotes, not recycled ones, and I do not want bland comments."

Doing Your Homework

Both Eric Newhouse and Sue Russell did plenty of home-work as an effective way to penetrate the shield thrown up by some sources. Come to the interview prepared with an understanding and knowledge of the issue, problem, or individual. Study up. Sift through back issues of your news-paper or magazine and go elsewhere for whatever informa-tion you need; the Internet can be mined as one source. Even the most hard-shelled interviewee is likely to warm up to a journalist who knows the score. David Perlman, a sci-ence writer for the *San Francisco Chronicle* and a past pres-ident of the National Association of Science Writers, says, "I've found that knowing something in general about the subject's work immediately establishes confidence. I try to get as much background as I can on the work the scientist has done in the past and is doing now."

Perlman tells of one scientist who confided: "Dave, I always like to talk to the media, but when a reporter comes to me and says, 'Doc, what's new in astronomy?' I freeze and cut the conversation as short as possible. But if the reporter shows that he knows something about the work I or others do, then I'm happy to explain things as clearly as possible."

Even experienced journalists sometimes miscue because of skimpy research. Doug Frantz, national projects editor for *The New York Times,* recalls in *Editor & Publisher* mag-azine that he regretted not having a better grasp of Scien-tology before interviewing leaders of that organization. At his first meeting with the officials, he goes on, he faced six lawyers, three top church officials, and a stenographer.

"They spent the first 45 minutes attacking me," Frantz says. "Needless to say, it got off on the wrong foot."

But Frantz's subsequent reporting on Scientology went much more smoothly and he explains why: "I honestly wish that I had understood Scientology better when I wrote the first story. By the time I had spent a year on the subject I was a lot smarter on every aspect of it." Frantz notes that religion is a particularly touchy topic, adding, "When investigating religions, expect hostility. Nobody likes their religious beliefs and practices questioned."

Know and Tell

A time-honored ploy for nudging recalcitrant sources out of their shell is to tell what you already know about the subject at hand. You may not know much but even a smidgen of information may convince the person that you know more than you actually do, thus prompting him to unload the rest. The maneuver doesn't always work but it beats going on a fishing expedition to pull out a story. If you have documentation to support your knowledge, don't hesitate to display it. But if you have only one copy, don't leave it with the interviewee.

If you don't have much on the matter at least familiarize yourself with the individual's recent past. In the event of a frozen silence, you might, for example, mention a recent talk he gave on the issue of the moment or refer to an award he received. Such a move may win him to your side. Moreover, prominent people, particularly, are often offended by reporters who know almost nothing about them beyond their name and position. Rapport is not always essential to an interview, although it usually makes it easier. Much of this information can be obtained from your publication's database or back issues. There are also handy reference books such as *Who's Who in America* and the *Dictionary of American Biography*. And don't forget the Internet.

Not knowing enough about the interviewee can be embarrassing as CNN talk show host Larry King learned on a New Year's Eve broadcast in 1999. He asked his guest, the Dalai Lama, if the year 2000 ushered in a millennium for him. "In the Muslim year, do you celebrate this as a year for your holy day?" King followed. The trouble was that the Dalai Lama is a Buddhist, forcing King to come back after a commercial to apologize for the error, which viewers had called in to correct.

A strong dose of sensitivity is a necessary ingredient for any interview. Don't become so absorbed in or enamored of your questions that you don't listen carefully to the person sitting across from you. Pick up on nuances in his conversation that may spark your next question. Be attuned to evasions or fear of candor. And don't form judgments or conceptions about an individual prior to meeting him for the first time. James "Scotty" Reston, of *The New York Times*, recounted in his memoirs an interview with Republican leader Sen. Robert Taft, who was reputed to be "stuffy, cheerless and calculating." But Reston found him "friendly, open-minded and almost boyishly happy."

At times during an interview, "Shut up and listen," advises IRE. "A good reporter is a good listener. You shouldn't be trying to tell people everything you know. You want to get what they know. Sometimes the best questions are 'Uh-huh,' 'Why?' 'How?' 'What do you mean?' and 'I don't understand,' the short questions which keep people talking, while you keep listening."

"Poor listening causes many newsroom mistakes, and editors and reporters share the blame," says writing coach Jim Stasiowski in *ANAgrams,* a publication of the Arizona Newspapers Association. "Reporters must learn to listen to their sources . . . Listen closely for the fact or opinion that steers you to some place you hadn't thought of going. Follow the path no one else has gone down."

Sometimes the problem in a dead-in-the-water interview lies not with the source but with the reporter. An unprepared questioner should not expect the other party to do his job for him. Starting the conversation with such overly broad queries like, "What can you tell me about interest rates?" is not likely to garner the subject's confidence in the asker's professionalism. To avoid such gaffes, go to the interview with six or seven prepared questions that target the main reason for the encounter and ask them in a direct, straightforward manner. Don't read the questions from your notebook. This not only dulls the spontaneity of the interview but might cause the interviewee to suspect that he's being set up. Rather, store the queries in your head before you leave your house or office, or as one reporter suggests, form them while taking a shower. The questions will inevitably lead to other questions suggested by the replies. In a few moments, the interview will be in full swing.

But remember that an interview is a two-way street. The IRE puts it this way: "You want your sources to be honest with you, don't you? Be honest with them if you want to build a mutual trust. That doesn't mean putting everything on a platter before the first question. But do try to be candid, rather than coy. If you're working on a story, say so. Take people part of the way into your confidence. Maybe they will do the same for you."

The interviewee's trust is more likely to come if you are at least partially conversant with the topic at hand.

"[W]e need people [in journalism] who have mastered their subjects, whether it is business news or computers or entertainment or local news," said Sandra Mims Rowe, editor of the Portland *Oregonian* and past president of the American Society of Newspaper Editors, in an *Editor & Publisher* interview. "The reason is that readers have become more sophisticated. Some of the public are very, very knowledgeable in particular areas and . . . immediately recognize the lack of authority and mastery in that area." Professionals in a particular area will, of course, be even more apt to spot lack of preparation.

Being prepared also can be an antidote for hostile or tight-lipped sources, journalists have found. "One technique I use is to bring up something I already know about the person or his family," discloses Henry C. Wiencek, author of the book, *The Hairstons: An American Family in Black and White,* which was featured on CBS' "60 Minutes" and later made into a TV miniseries. "Then they know I am a serious researcher and that I already am interested in their story." It worked well for his book—a history of a slave-owning family in the South—Wiencek attests. "They would say something, either to correct me or to amplify material I had," he says. "Very often people who are hostile to you will reveal a great deal of information they wouldn't otherwise give out. They want to put you in your place. So it's important that you go into an interview having as much background about the person as possible. And don't be afraid of making mistakes. Sometimes an uninformed question can call forth a lot of useful information."

The Pitfall of Yes and No Answers

As Cindy Yorks warned, a sure way to wind up with no story is to allow an interviewee to answer only yes or no to your questions. The source may indeed be a shy or close-mouthed character, but the wooden response is often the reporter's fault for not broadening the interrogation. Such an exchange may go like this between a reporter and the chief of the city's sanitation department:

"Mr. Chambers, a lot of residents are saying your department could have prevented the sewer backup. Is that true?"

"No."

"Are you taking any steps to prevent this happening again?"

"Yes."

"Were you aware that the sewer drain on Foster Street had been clogged up for several weeks?"

"No."

"Don't crews go out and check drains?"

"Yes."

Such answers, of course, will lead to a blank notebook or tape, to say nothing about an embarrassing meeting with your editor. Chambers probably isn't happy about being put on the spot over the sewer mess but, as a public official, he is responsible to the public. So make him aware of his responsibility by asking open-end questions that will elicit real-time facts to which readers and viewers are entitled. The first question might be phrased: "Mr. Chambers, what's your feeling about all the criticism about the way your department maintains the sewer system?" The next question might be, "What steps are you taking to prevent this from happening again?" This could be followed by, "How often are the drains serviced and who is in charge of that job?" The idea is to prevent a source from wiggling off the hook by a yes or no reply. Politely but insistently broaden the questioning to the point that he cannot fob off a yes or no answer.

A Matter of Self-Interest

Newsmakers don't give interviews for the press' benefit. Self-interest is usually a motivating factor. Even so, some sources will, on controversial issues, stubbornly skirt around meaningful rejoinders to questions. This may be the time to suggest that she will further her own cause or that of her organization by being more forthcoming. If there is a societal benefit that might come from frank responses—clean government, disease prevention, narcotics control, and so on—mention that as well. But be careful not to intimate that you share her convictions—even if you do—or are there as an advocate for her objectives.

The late Clark Mollenhoff, a Pulitzer Prize-winner who achieved fame as a Washington correspondent for the *Des Moines Register,* recalled in his book *Investigative Reporting* (Macmillan, 1981) that as a young reporter in Iowa he was assigned to interview a garage owner who was accused in a scheme to "outrageously" overcharge the county for repair of its vehicles. The man had a mean disposition and did not welcome reporters prying into his activities. When Mollenhoff and his photographer confronted the 250-pound suspect in his garage he was wielding a tire iron with which he threatened to smash their heads. But eventually Mollenhoff was able to extract a wealth of information from him by playing to his pent-up feelings. Wrote Mollenhoff: "Croft . . . did not consider himself as bad as his conspirators. He had convinced himself that he had been sucked into unethical acts by others [and] felt that he was being made 'the fall guy' for those who profited most from the frauds on the county treasury. Probably Croft was motivated to give the interview by a desire to express those considerations." Before the interview, Mollenhoff had dug deeply into the case and was thus armed to exploit Croft's vulnerabilities.

Fortunately, most interviews are carried out without the danger of bodily harm to journalists but it can happen. The author once went to interview a labor organizer who, as it turned out, had a long-standing grudge against the writer's newspaper. When the latter introduced himself, the union leader grabbed him by the lapels of his jacket, snarling, "I wouldn't give that rag you work for the time of day." After a few moments, however, he calmed down and vented his spleen on a company whose employees he was trying to unionize. The author was able to convince him that he had come as an objective reporter who wanted to hear the union side of the dispute, having already talked to a management representative.

Often a successful interview requires common sense on the part of the journalist. People should be treated as you would want to be treated under similar circumstances. The reporter who pursues his or her task with the idea that their position gives them the right to be arrogant and condescending may go away empty-handed. Sweeping as it is, the First Amendment does not force anyone to talk to the media. Even the president of the United States is not required to hold news conferences or submit to interviews (some presidents have been noted for their long gaps between press conferences). The best approach to any interview is to be well mannered and sensitive to what may be an ordeal for the subject. "Over the years, people have told me they talked to me because I don't approach them like a 'story,'" Karen Saunders, an award-winning producer for the ABC-TV program "20/20," told a *Columbia Journalism Review* reporter about her interviewing technique. "I approach them as another person. I'll give people time to think. You can't push in on somebody. Treat people as human beings and it is more than likely that they will respond." What she is saying, in essence, is don't be confrontational, a dictum followed by many top-ranked journalists. Yet, it should be stressed here that neither should you let yourself be pushed around by a source. Don't match him in invective or insults—should they be delivered—but stand your ground and try to convince him that you are a professional doing your job and have no axe to grind. If he still insists on being nasty, you may take some comfort in the fact that his utterances, however unpleasant, can be woven into your story or broadcast. Actually, most public figures, whatever their feelings toward the media, are savvy enough not to vent their spleen on the reporter in front of them.

The Benefits Appeal

Interviews can go much easier when the subject is eager to get his story out for the good that it can do—either for himself or others. In a piece about fraudulent telemarketers preying on elderly people in the *Santa Barbara* (California) *News-Press,* reporter Che Tabisola interviewed a man who had been swindled out of $25,000 by a phone scammer. Despite the fact that he felt like a "sitting duck," the victim talked freely, calling the experience a "good lesson." Seniors can protect themselves from similar losses by heeding the man's tale, the story pointed out.

Because they believe others will benefit from their loss or gain, some interviewees will cooperate with a journalist. But if not, an appeal to their sense of the public good may open the spigot. Such an approach has enabled reporters to extract quotes from fire and robbery victims, hostages, AIDS patients, and lung cancer sufferers. This also can work with scientists, business leaders, or school officials who may be reluctant to face the press. A diabetes researcher, for example, may be persuaded to debunk an unproven drug for the disease if it's brought home to him that his expertise could prevent scores of people from being at risk by using the medicine.

Of course, you will have the easiest time with those whose job it is to hand out advice and warnings: forest rangers, fire chiefs, police officers, state and local consumer department spokespersons, school nurses, State Department officials, and so on.

A word of caution: deal gently with persons who have gone through a traumatic experience. They may indeed be willing to speak in the interest of helping others, but don't rush them into it or suggest that they have an humanitarian obligation to unload themselves. They don't. First gain their confidence. Then build up to your key questions. And if the words finally spill out in torrents, let them flow. You can always go back and fill in the gaps or ask for a repetition of what you didn't get.

Return Engagement

The old adage, "If at first you don't succeed, try try again" is applicable to some interviews. Like most of us, interview subjects have bad days and one of them could be on your scheduled time. She may have gotten unpleasant news before your arrival; she may not have slept well the night before or is bothered by a cold. In any case, the interview is not going well and there is little chance it will improve. If it's not a breaking story, show your understanding of her discomfort by suggesting another time, perhaps the next day. You might have to move up your deadline, but the second meeting is likely to produce a better piece because the atmosphere has changed. You are not fighting something over which you have no control. Feature and profile interviews are covered in detail in another chapter but it can be noted here that in profiling certain people, a reporter may spend three or four days with them, including being a guest in their homes.

In his book, *Freelance Writing: Advice from the Pros,* veteran author Curtis Casewit tells of the time he interviewed a German scientist famous for his work in cellular therapy. In two one-hour interviews, the man offered almost nothing. On his third effort, Casewit brought up the fact that the American Medical Association took a dim view of his experiments. "The professor finally began to talk, explaining why the AMA was wrong, and he went on from there," Casewit wrote.

Of course, even a one-day delay is impractical for a breaking story. Even if the main subject is less than forthcoming for whatever reason, you must meet your deadline. In this case, get what you can and try to buttress the story with other sources. It's a good idea to call the newsmaker a day or two in advance to make sure he remembers the date and will be available.

"Ambush" Interviewing

Media critics—and there are many—often single out the so-called ambush interview when denouncing what in their view is contemptible journalism. In the worst-case scenario of such practice, a reporter and photographer surprise a victim in the driveway of his home, a nightclub, or in one case, a hospital, as actor Alec Baldwin and his wife were leaving one with their baby. This is the trashiest kind of tabloid journalism, say these critics. The *Columbia Journalism Review,* which regularly chronicles the good and the bad of American journalism, comments: "The image of the hard-boiled journalist, callously lying in wait with camera or notebook to accost the tragically grief-stricken, has moved from cliché to caricature to symbol of our business." The condemnations often involve suddenly confronting people in sorrow after the death of a child or spouse, or of minor children. Aghast over what it termed a media invasion of the privacy of Caroline Kennedy Schlossberg and her young children after the plane-crash death of her brother, John F. Kennedy Jr., *Brill's Content,* another media watchdog publication, called on major news organizations to voluntarily refrain from publishing photos of family members immediately after the death of a loved one or children under the age of 14 without permission. Predictably, the press overwhelmingly rejected the idea, preferring instead to examine the issue on a case-by-case basis.

The issue is a serious one but should be put in perspective. By far, the most egregious of these offenses are committed by the supermarket tabloid papers whose passion for sensationalism has few bounds. Let's also leave room here for certain television stations whose take-no-prisoners style of reporting disgusts many viewers. Unfortunately, the public usually makes no distinction between these culprits and the mainstream press. Although the latter is not entirely without blemish in the matter, their transgressions are miniscule compared to the flashy tabloids and frantic TV camera crews.

The plain truth of journalism is that sometimes a reporter must wait awhile at an outside or inside location to obtain a news interview. Perhaps the subject refuses to see reporters at his office or home. Maybe the person is moving around so much and so fast that it's virtually impossible to set up a formal interview. Or it could be that the source is in a closed meeting and not available until he emerges. As mentioned earlier, reporters are not admitted into grand jury rooms and so must catch lawyers as they come out during breaks. If it's a legitimate news story, don't have qualms about such tactics. It's your job to get the story, giving the public its right to know. There also may be times when it is necessary to approach grieving parents or others in emotional distress. Do it tactfully. Be compassionate and understanding. Empathize by imagining yourself in such a situation. Identify yourself and explain your job. You may be surprised at their willingness to talk to you. Just don't hide behind bushes and leap out at unsuspecting victims; your reception may be less than cordial.

Put the Questions in the Mail

To avoid a confrontation with a writer some sources demand that questions be submitted to them in writing. This is not the best way to conduct an interview; in fact, it's close to being the worst. For one thing, there is virtually no opportunity for the vital follow-up questions when the initial answer falls short of telling you what you want to know. If you're on a tight deadline there is no assurance that the individual will get his responses to you in time. Also, there is no opportunity to weave color into your article, such as the decor of his or her office or home, what they're wearing, mannerisms, and so on. A personality profile is hardly possible under such circumstances. In journalism, however, reporters often must play with the cards they are dealt. If the interview is important and the person insists on a long-distance arrangement, go along. It's better than no interview. More than one story has emerged from such communication. Be sure though to submit a lot of questions on the theory that your respondent will toss out some he doesn't like. And if the replies don't add up to a coherent story, you might try phoning him or her to fill in the holes, stressing his stake in an accurate account.

When more than one subject is required to flesh out an article, you may have to resort to a copying machine. Ten respondents, say, get the same questionnaire and hopefully will respond in time for your deadline. Laggards may require a follow-up letter, e-mail, or phone plea. The list should include a cover note to explain its purpose.

Okay, You've Crashed through the Barrier

Reporter Sally Steadfast has overcome the subject's initial resistance and the interview proceeds. Are her problems over? Not by a longshot. She must keep the process going, even when the interviewee balks at certain questions, goes off on nonresponsive discourses, or evades direct answers. When a query gets a stonewall reception, it sometimes helps to rephrase it to make it more palatable. Instead of asking the mayor, "Did you use your city credit card to book a Caribbean cruise for you and your family?" you might try, "Mr. Mayor, are the allegations true that you made personal purchases with your official credit card?" The cruise might be the next question.

Some subjects are given to irrelevant rambling, which should be allowed to go only so far. A person caught up in a childhood memory, for example, can usually be returned to the present with a polite intervention, such as: "That is very interesting, Dr. Bradshaw, but could we get back to what you were saying a few moments ago about the fascination of UFOs?" However, as noted elsewhere in this book, some writers, particularly in a profile, believe in letting a subject digress to an extent in the hope that he or she will bring forth a usable nugget. Sometimes it does.

One method of dealing with evasive replies is to share with the person what you already know about the matter at hand, including what others may have said about it. This is a classic means of opening him up. Another way is to tell him that his dodging the issue or fudging the facts will be noted in your story, perhaps creating doubts about his character and reliability. This works best with politicians and other public figures. Be tough when you have to—without engaging in arguments or an exchange of viewpoints. In an interview, you are not supposed to have a viewpoint if you want to maintain your professionalism.

If, on the other hand, relevant words are flowing from the individual like a tidal wave, it may be best to halt the questioning for awhile and let her talk. "A reporter doesn't have to be asking questions all the time," says *Anchorage* (Alaska) *Daily News* reporter Larry Campbell, a member of a Pulitzer Prize-winning writing team. "Americans seem to be afraid of silence," he observes. "But keeping your mouth shut at the right times allows the other senses to work." In his remarks to newspaper writing coaches, Campbell added: "In an interview, when the reporter stops, that is a clear sign to whoever is being interviewed that it's his or her turn. I sit still and observe while they worry about filling the silence. It took me some time to get into the habit. But when I saw the dividends in better stories, knowing when to shut up became easy."

Los Angeles Times' national correspondent John Balzar had a similar experience in interviewing movie director Oliver Stone, who paused frequently in the session, sometimes during mid-sentence. Describing the meeting at one point, Balzar writes: "The next hour passes slowly, even painfully—strained, or, if you choose, illuminated by Stone's rocket flights of thought . . . Stone continues, his inflections and pauses dramatic." The writer's patience paid off in a compelling profile of Stone and his views on the Vietnam war in which he fought, and filmmaking.

Another writer who isn't concerned about an occasional dead spot in an interview is *Dayton Daily News* columnist Mary McCarty. "Don't be afraid of silences because interview subjects might say something worth waiting for if you briefly delay asking the next question," she related to *Editor & Publisher.* In the same article, Susan Ager, a *Detroit Free Press* columnist, advised: "The more relaxed you make people feel, the more they'll tell you."

Many celebrities have a low threshold for questions they've been asked time and time again by reporters and may want to cut the interview short out of sheer boredom. George Varga, pop music critic for the *San Diego Union-Tribune,* says he's ready for that.

"I do my homework by preparing questions he or she might not have been asked," he relates. "In fact, I start by suggesting that the person must be tired of hearing the same old questions from journalists. Then I bring up something they probably have not been asked before. This usually gets them started." Varga recollects that the strategem worked well with Playboy founder Hugh Hefner at a time when the Playboy Foundation was sponsoring a music festival. "I asked him about his tastes in music, which came as a surprise to him since he's usually dealing with queries about his lifestyle and the Playboy girls. It turned out to be a really good interview."

"Let's Meet for Lunch"

Sound like a good idea for an interview? Indeed, it can be. Scads of interviews are conducted in restaurants, coffee shops, bars, and even pizza parlors. The locale has its advantages. Your subject may be more relaxed in an informal setting than in his office or home and thus more likely to speak openly and frankly. Also, there probably will be fewer or no interruptions because of phone calls, office problems, kids playing, or the dog wandering into the room. If, however, the source is carrying a cell phone the conversation could be sidetracked if he accepts calls.

But beware of the negative aspects of such cozy surroundings. If you're using a tape recorder in a restaurant for example, background noises of chattering diners, clattering plates, waiters' spiels, electric fans, or air conditioning can play havoc with your cassette's sound capabilities and be generally distracting. The author once interviewed a TV star, who insisted on meeting at his favorite breakfast place in a posh Los Angeles neighborhood. The interview went well. The actor was voluble, charming, and didn't duck any questions. But the tape was a near disaster. The cafe was a popular local hangout and was jammed at the time. The playback picked up the high noise level, which drowned out almost half of what the source said, requiring a call to him the next day to fill in the missing pieces. Notes were taken but the bulk of the replies were recorded.

The experience provided a valuable lesson, which is passed on here. If your interview date is in a restaurant and you plan to tape it, try to pick a lone table in a corner, away from the main throng of customers. If it's a lunch meeting, aim for a time when the crowd has thinned out, say 1:30 or 2 P.M. If a restaurant or coffee house has patio tables, head for one (in good weather of course). The din is likely to be much less. And have a high-quality tape recorder and cassettes, which should be tested out before the interview. The authors do not recommend microcassette recorders for interviews in noisy places. The bigger the equipment the better. Incidentally, some restaurant reviewers mention the sound level of the establishment; the review could be worth clipping for future reference.

A final note on restaurant interviews: pick up the check even if the subject offers to. You don't want to feel obligated to him or her because of a free meal, nor do you want them to expect favorable treatment in return for the same. Most news organizations provide reporters with expense accounts for such occasions. Many magazines also will foot the bill for freelancers it assigns for articles. But be sure to keep the receipt, which you may have to show. And even if you are not reimbursed, the receipts are necessary if you claim tax deductions as a writer. In the matter of expense accounts, it's a good idea to ask the editor for one before undertaking an assignment.

DOs and DON'Ts of Interviewing

DO:
- Go into the interview with an open mind.
- Have at least five prepared questions to start off.
- Ask questions in plain language.

- Keep them as short as possible; avoid getting tangled up in long-winded or two- or three-part questions.
- Rephrase or cut out jargon and arcane words if the subject has trouble understanding your question.
- Maintain eye contact with the interviewee as often as you can while taking notes (good reason for using a tape recorder).
- Dress properly for the occasion so you will be taken seriously. Jeans and sportshirts are out, although women can wear dressy slacks. Tie and jacket for men.
- Ask follow-up questions when necessary to clarify or expand on an utterance.
- Ask the person to suggest others who might have information or opinions on the subject at hand. If she does, push your luck for their phone numbers. If you're doing a personality profile, request names of friends, relatives, schoomates, ex-wives, business associates, and so on.
- Stop the questions if the individual becomes agitated or seems to need time to collect his thoughts. A momentary lapse won't hurt the interview.
- Be in control of the interview. Don't let the subject take charge.
- Wind up an interview by asking the source if he or she wants to comment on anything not covered in the questions. It may open a whole new area.
- Get phone numbers where the individual can be reached, particularly if he or she is planning an out-of-town trip in the next few days.

DON'T:

- Go to your source with a preconceived notion of what you'll hear.
- Arrive late for the assignment.
- Call your source by his or her first name unless invited to.
- Begin the interview with a tough, controversial or embarrassing question. Warm up the atmosphere with a few innocuous comments or observations (Is that a picture of your family?). Go for the vital stuff when you're well underway. Otherwise, it may be a very brief meeting.
- Waste too much time on small talk; it's not a social affair.
- Engage in arguments with the person or express your own views on the subject. An interview is not a debate.
- Agree with his views. This can create an impression that your article will be favorable to him. There's no harm, however, in admiring a book he authored, a play in which he appeared, or the decor of his home or office.
- Ask the interviewee if you can quote her. This could give her repressive ideas. If she wants something off the record, she will probably say so. Assume that everything said is quotable unless told otherwise; even then you can try to convince her the statement should be printed. But be careful of publishing potentially libelous remarks.
- Be afraid to ask the painful questions. The answers make news.
- Leave without understanding any part of what was said.
- Leave before getting phone numbers if the source plans to be away during your writing time.
- Forget you notes, tape recorder, and documents you may have been given.

6

The Phone: An Essential Tool

How could the media exist without the telephone? It's too horrible to contemplate but once they did. Civil War correspondents used the telegraph for their dispatches from the battlefields, a practice that generals and government officials on both sides attempted to squelch, fearing that news provided key information to the enemy. In 1861, Secretary of State William H. Seward ordered military censors to forbid all telegraphic dispatches from Washington relating to military and civil operations. In pre-phone days, newspapers also used messengers and even pigeons to relay news. In colonial days, journalists rowed out from New York and Boston Harbors to meet ships arriving from Europe so they could be first with the news from abroad.

Today, the telephone is like an appendage to a journalist's arm. The main reasons are speed and access. Staffers on a daily newspapers often simply don't have the time to visit a source for an interview and still meet their deadline. At other times, the subject may be unavailable for a face-to-face meeting. The phone also is frequently indispensable to television and radio reporters and magazine and freelance writers. Currently, a cell phone is as much a part of a journalist's baggage as a pen and notebook.

Today's fast-paced reporting frequently doesn't allow for close-encounter interviews—to say nothing about the problems of distance. After 19-year-old Eric Burns pleaded guilty in federal court to computer hacking, an Associated Press reporter in the Washington, D.C., bureau phoned him at his home in Shorewood, Washington, to get his reaction to his crime and the 15-month sentence. High up in the story was Burns' comment that, "I didn't really think it was too much of a big deal."

Phone Protocol

Rarely are phone interviews scheduled in advance. Unlike their arrangements for an office or home interview, reporters grab a telephone for what are usually quick conversations aimed at squaring away a story, getting a needed quote, confirming a report, or finding additional sources. But speed and necessity cannot be excuses for bungling an interview through a wrong approach.

In talking to a source you know and who knows you, a minimum of preliminaries are required. But when the person on the other end of the line is a stranger, think differently. First, always identify yourself and your publication—not, "This is the Daily Trumpet," but "This is Joe Davis from the Daily Trumpet." Don't—whatever the circumstances—pretend to be a cop, social worker, IRS agent, or any other figure as a means of tapping into a skittish source. The lie can get both you and your employer in trouble, including triggering a lawsuit.

If you want to tape the interview, ask the source's permission. Several states have statutes governing phone taping and it's a wise idea to check the rule in your state. Fran Carpentier urges writers to use a tape recorder for both phone and in-person interviews. "When you play the tape," she explains, "you not only get the words but a sense of the individual's personality and charisma."

In collecting material for a book or magazine article, there may be less of a rush, allowing you to better prepare yourself and providing the time to become more acquainted with your sources. Veteran journalists have learned to take a measured approach in conversing with people they can't see and who can't see them.

Dan Hurley establishes his credibility by immediately stating what publication he is writing for in connection with the interview. "I say, for example, that I'm working on an article for *Family Circle* magazine and start firing away, even if I may not yet have an assignment for *Family Circle*. But I feel it's okay to state this because I would actually be gathering material for a query to that publication." In fact, Hurley's byline has appeared in *Family Circle*.

In general, Hurley reveals, he would rather interview experts on the phone "but if there is a human interest component, I want to meet the person."

It's difficult to convey a person's personality from a phone conversation—particularly if you have not met him or her—but inklings can emerge for a feature article if there is no chance of face-to-face contact. If the source hesitates or seems evasive over some questions, this can be part of your report. If he yells at you or laughs uproariously after a question, slip it in your piece. If he uses colorful language, flavor can be added to your story, although the insertion of cuss words will depend on the policy of your publication.

The Pros and Cons of Phone Interviews

Besides saving precious time, the phone may cause the source to be more voluble. In contrast to a visible interview, from which some subjects may shy away, the telephone allows a remoteness that lets them be at ease. People use the phone all day long so one more call may not make that much difference, even from a journalist. You also may be saving *his* time, which he may appreciate. And if the called party is not a regular newsmaker, he might welcome the break in his daily routine. The authors have found many ordinary citizens willing to talk to them on the phone—an exception may be when the story concerns a personal tragedy. You may be their first caller of the day.

"Much of your interviewing will of necessity be by telephone and usually on deadline," Joseph Galloway of *U.S. News & World Report* points out. "But you must never get in such a hurry that you forget to listen to both what is said and what is meant. Your search is not only for the truth but also for details that enlighten and brighten any story. Be polite; be friendly; you should be upfront about who you are and why you are calling. Be a good listener always. It is the nature of people that they want to share what they know; they want to tell you what you want to know. Don't get in the way of letting them do that."

The downside of phone interviewing is the hesitancy— and perhaps suspicion—that some people have in talking to strangers. Remember, there are all kinds of frauds perpetrated via the telephone, and you may be unfortunate enough to be taken for one of the con artists. There also are those who don't like the media and react accordingly. Also, some people do not immediately grasp the name of the caller and his purpose. More then one reporter has been told by someone at the other end of the line that she already subscribes to the paper.

These are reasons to be extra persuasive with the speaker. Besides identifying yourself and your publication, invite the person to phone your office to authenticate your identity if doubts are raised. In their book *All the President's Men,* which chronicled their famed Watergate investigation, Bob Woodward and Carl Bernstein tell of the former's call to Kenneth H. Dahlberg in Minneapolis, who figured in the case. At first, Dahlberg refused to discuss a $25,000 check about which he was questioned. He hung up. But he called back a few minutes later, saying he had balked at replying to Woodward's queries because he wasn't really sure that he was a *Washington Post* reporter. Dahlberg then responded freely to Woodward's questions. It also helped that Woodward already had some background information on the check, thus prompting Dahlberg to fill in the blanks.

Consider also that the time you are calling may be inconvenient for your party. She may be in a meeting, rushing off to the dentist, or talking on another phone. Ask politely when you can call back. If you're on a tight deadline, say so to hopefully speed the process. Don't count on *her* to phone you, even if she promises to. The call is probably more important to you than to her. Shirley Camper Soman says her approach is to "first tell who I am and then ask if this is a good time. I make sure of the timing. It's very important. If the time is bad, I ask for another telephone date when they are available. This gesture has led to some incredibly fine interviews."

Although preparation is vital to any interview, it is especially important on the phone. "You have a limited amount of time," notes Jeannine Stein, a *Los Angeles Times* columnist and feature writer. "Do your homework. Thoroughly research whatever biographical or background you need. Be ready with penetrating questions and follow-ups. If the person knows that you know your stuff, it's more likely they'll trust you and feel more comfortable talking to you."

Stein also points out that phone interviews often are a "one-shot deal. There's no chance for a second interview because of time—yours or their's—or distance. So make sure you get all the information you need." Stein adds that she saves questions that might make the subject uncomfortable for the very end. "That way," she reasons, "if they hang up on you, you will still have quotes."

Getting by the Gatekeeper

Secretaries or other aides standing between you and your source can ruin your day or enhance it. Some secretaries seem to regard protecting their boss from reporters as a kind of crusade. Others are reasonably accommodating—unless you start throwing your weight around with demands in the name of a free press. The press is free but so is the secretary or personal assistant—free to keep you away from her employer or free to hang up on you. So, whether on the phone or face-to-face, be polite, be friendly. Don't yell, be condescending, or treat him or her as an inferior being. If the source is someone you will have to contact on a regular basis, be especially intent on establishing a cordial relationship with his or her office staffers.

There will be times when, whether the aide is cooperative or not, your target will not be in. She may be out of town on business, at a managerial retreat, on vacation, taking a shower or working at home. You, however, must meet a deadline and can't wait until she returns. First, ask for a number where she can be reached. If that fails, inquire if she will be calling her office. If so, leave your phone numbers—saying them slowly and clearly—where she can reach you, whether it's your home or office or at-large by cellular transmission. Often this works. The author recalls one source who called him from an airport minutes before his plane took off, yet remained on the line long enough to answer all necessary questions. If you have interviewed a subject and know there will be additional questions based on your further research, try to get the person's away-from-home number or at least the name of the hotel or other place where he or she may be staying. This request is usually granted since the source is apt to be just as interested as you in an accurate, complete story. The advent of cellular phones has, happily, made contact easier. Many reporters have gotten calls from newsmakers in their cars, on the street, and in restaurants. If you have a cell phone, communication can be even more effective.

Crossing Countries and Continents

Cross-country and overseas calls are routine for major media. But small newspapers, magazines, and broadcast stations also have used long-distance wire to advantage. Sometimes, this route is easier than local calls in search of information. Many officials and ordinary citizens are flattered by getting a call from a publication or station hundreds or thousands of miles away. They may talk more readily than they would to their hometown paper or station.

But whatever their reaction, the call may be absolutely necessary to round out a story when a close-up interview is impossible because of time and distance. Prize-winning reporter Eileen Welsome of the *Albuquerque* (New Mexico) *Tribune* was both resourceful and persistent in gathering material via several phone calls for her story and a subsequent book (*The Plutonium Files,* Delacorte) about secret U.S. medical experiments on human beings during the Cold War. In one instance, the only clue to one of the victims was that he might have been from a small town in Texas. She found the town on a map and first called its city hall to learn the identity of the man, who was only given a code number by government scientists. Welsome described the individual to a clerk, who identified him immediately. The journalist learned the names of two other patients by calling one of the researchers in the experiments. All three had died, but Welsome gleaned facts by contacting relatives, funeral homes, and cemetery offices, eventually connecting five deceased persons to the plutoniuim testing. Her awards for the project included the coveted $25,000 Selden Ring Award for investigative reporting.

Communicating Via the Internet

Science writer William Allen of the *St. Louis Post-Dispatch* points out that the newspaper has found the Internet valuable in collecting information for several stories, including an interview with physicist Ernst Zimmer and Kenyan scientist Florence Wambugu. Not only can a reporter touch base with a source (if he is online), but she also can punch into several Web sites loaded with information on scores of subjects. These include MEDNEWS for science and medical news releases; AP ONLINE, an abbreviated form of the Associated Press' wire service on America Online and Compu-Serve; and Electronic Mail, another Compu-Serve service that enables you to send messages and transfer files to millions of users.

Sending an e-mail letter to a source may prompt a quick reply, even from someone who has not returned your calls. The same can hold true for facsimile transmission. In this technological age when it seems every third person has a computer and is packing a cellular phone, electronic is often the way to go. Your source's e-mail and fax data may be on his business card but, if not, ask for them. And be sure to give him your electronic address. Freelancers should have business cards with the above information. E-mail and faxes are not as effective as a one-on-one interview, but in some circumstances you have to take whatever route you can.

Calling the Guy Next Door

Breaking stories demand fast phone work, but that doesn't help if there is nobody on the other end of the line or your party can't or won't pick up the phone. You must think fast as well. Imagine a fire tearing through a nursing home. Before reporters and photographers can get to the scene you have to get enough information to write a first edition story or get something on the wire or on air. The building is being evacuated and firefighters will not stop their efforts to answer phones—assuming they are even working. You do the next best thing—call homes or businesses near the blaze for eyewitness reports. You may be surprised at how cooperative and observant some nonprofessionals can be. Telephone companies issue reverse directories—sometimes called in newspaper offices the "backward book." In these volumes, street addresses are listed before the names of subscribers, enabling you to find an address close to the scene of an accident or fire. You might even get a next-door neighbor.

In long-distance situations, similar strategies may be required as demonstrated by Eileen Welsome. Individuals whose numbers or addresses you don't have may be reached by calling a local phone company, city hall, the tax assessor, gas company or the Chamber of Commerce if he or she is in business. If you know any friend, classmate, business associate, ex-spouse, fraternity brother, or fellow club member, ring them up if you have a number. If the person is known to be a golfer, fitness buff, theater-goer, horseman, art collector, and so on, try golf clubs, gyms, theater groups, and galleries to see if he has an address or phone number.

The *New York Times* found a source who literally lived next door to one of the suspects in a sweep by federal officials of 18 persons in North Carolina suspected of trafficking in contraband cigarettes to raise funds for Hezbollah, regarded by the U.S. government as a terrorist group in the Middle East. The man was quoted liberally as saying he had had no idea his neighbor was involved in criminal activity, calling him a "nice guy, a regular guy." Obviously, such a source lends human interest in what otherwise is a rather standard story of a police raid.

"I'll Get Back to You"

Don't take this statement at face value. A source may indeed have a reason for not speaking to you at the moment and really intends to call you back. It does happen but don't bank on it, particularly if you're on a deadline. Try to pin down a time for her response, stressing your deadline. When a reasonable period has elapsed, call the subject again and leave an "urgent" message on her voice machine, if she has one. If you eventually fear her promise was a stalling ploy and that no call is coming, phone again with another message, offering to discuss any misgivings she might have about talking for publication. You might also point out that others involved in the story have spoken, assuming they have. If you're still drawing zeroes, phone people close to her, co-workers, relatives, and so on. Ask them to persuade her to ring you up. Use any legitimate means you can to get the interview. An editor will not be pleased to hear that you struck out. However, if the attempt does end in failure, be sure to note in your story that she declined to be interviewed. At least the reader or viewer knows you tried. CBS's "60 Minutes" always notes that it sought but failed to obtain a response from a particular source in a controversial report.

The process can be frustrating, even when there are designated spokespersons, whose main job is to deal with the media. Reporters waited eagerly for the university president to announce the fate of Indiana University basketball coach Bobby Knight, who was accused of choking one of his players. The press also wanted a statement from Knight and phoned his office. Callers were referred to a spokesman for Indiana's basketball program. He did not return calls. When this happens reporters go after other sources, which is what The Associated Press did in this case. One man, identified only as a "top university official," was quoted as saying that Knight would keep his job under "strict conditions." An identified assistant to Knight predicted the coach would stay. AP's lead on its story cited "reports" that Knight would remain as coach if he agreed to "curb his infamous temper." Their tips turned out to be true. But weeks later, Knight was fired.

Patience Pays Off

The lesson is, try very hard before throwing in the towel. Stay on the phone until victory is yours. In another effort, George Varga of the *San Diego Union-Tribune* made phone calls to New York for several weeks seeking an interview with the pop group The Monkees before an upcoming concert in the San Diego area. "Their office didn't say yes and they didn't say no," recalls Varga. "There was one woman who took most of my calls and she kept putting me off. One day I had a nice bouquet of flowers sent to her. The next day she phoned me, saying I didn't have to do that. But I got the interview the following week." The same kind of persistence got Varga an interview with pop star Jimmy Buffett, who seldom grants them. "It was the only print interview he had done that year his manager told me," Varga notes.

Similar doggedness paid off for Gerald Posner, a lawyer-turned-writer, who was determined to obtain an interview with billionaire businessman and maverick politician Ross Perot for a biography of the man. The latter was just as determined not to give him one. Recapping the effort in *Writer's Digest,* Posner says he was told by Perot's press secretary that the tycoon preferred not to "waste" his time with print interviews, preferring television through which he could reach a larger audience. Perot also was fearful of having his printed quotes distorted.

"Forget it, he won't talk to you," the aide said.

Meanwhile, Posner continued interviewing other sources for the book, including Perot's son-in-law about Perot's POW-MIA activities. This brought an angry call from Perot to Posner about the interview and Posner's motives. More hostile calls followed in which the writer was asked if he represented the Republican or Democratic parties (Perot had been a Reform party presidential candidate), and challenged Posner to say whether the book would deal with "gossip and trivia."

"I listened, vigorously defended my work and did not back down," Posner says. "Once Perot realized he was not going to bully me into abandoning the project, he had to decide whether he wanted a serious biography of him published without any of his own contributions." The upshot was that Posner was invited to Dallas for an interview with "no subject off limits." The author of seven books and dozens of articles, Posner confides that his strategy is to begin any new project "guided by the need to look for innovative timing; the persistence to pursue every interview and document; and the desire to ensure that I always maintain my independence and journalistic integrity."

Need more inspiration? Successful freelancer Lawrence Grobel reminisces in *Writer's Digest* that it took him a year to meet singer-actress Barbra Streisand, months of negotiation, with countless phone calls, to get her to agree for a *Playboy* interview, "and nine more months passed before the interview was completed and I was paid." Subsequently, the magazine had gotten Marlon Brando to sit down for an interview and assigned Grobel to the job, which took less time but still required further negotiation with the actor. Top celebrities and their handlers choose interviewers and publications very carefully. But once you establish a reputation for such reporting, as did Grobel, assignments are likely to flow in.

7

Interviewing for Features

Unlike a breaking news event, a feature story often seems to have no clear focus. An editor might tell you to profile the admissions officer at a university charged with recruiting minorities, or send you out to write about a snake having surgery or a potato that looks like Liza Minnelli or a poodle party where owners dress their dogs like children. Or maybe she wants you to do a feature about fraternity or sorority rush or rape awareness week. First off, find an angle, or a focus. That focus should be on the humans behind the story—their quirks and foibles, their frailties and strengths, their weirdness and their passions. Readers and viewers relate best to people, not to abstract events, buildings, or legislation. If you're assigned to do a story about an ordinance to tear down the city's only senior housing and replace it with a shopping mall, go interview the soon-to-be homeless old lady clutching her cat. Where will they go? What will they do?

The Liza Minnelli potato becomes the news hook that gets you into the life of the farmer who found it, just as a story about rush should focus on the people going through it. Find the women and men in charge of rape awareness week—are they victims? Why have they devoted their time to making people aware of rape? And who are these people who dress their dogs like children and throw them parties? Why do they do it? What's their motivation?

Finding out why people behave the way they do—their motivation—is crucial to writing an insightful feature story. Ask questions that begin with "Why: Why did you start the rape awareness week event? Why did you want to join a fraternity?" Most people will toss off a prepared response or a message. Keep asking questions that begin with why, what, and how until you get to the place in your sources' past that brought them to where they are today. That's when you start getting close to understanding their motivation.

Motivation might stem from some obstacle in the past that your source has had to overcome, or is struggling to overcome. Find out what that obstacle is, and what bearing it has on your source's present behavior. Get specific examples and anecdotes. "Try not to qualify your question by asking for the most difficult problem or the funniest or happiest moment. People have difficulty deciding what is best, worst, hardest, easiest, happiest or saddest," warns veteran feature writer Carol Rich in her book *Writing and Reporting News: A Coaching Method.*

Did struggling to overcome the obstacle teach your source lessons that he or she is now using to deal with another problem or controversy? What did your source learn from the struggle? How did she learn it? Chronicle the struggle; these are the sorts of details you'll use to show readers—instead of telling them—how your source came to be in the spotlight of your story. Go to the story with a focus in mind, but remember to be willing to change your focus if the source takes you to a better place.

Finding Your Focus

The first step, then, is to find your focus. As with news stories, preparation is crucial. Find out everything you can ahead of time—given time constraints—about the source and the issue or event you're covering. If you're doing a story about a business, find out who their big competitors are and talk to them. If your source has been in trouble with the law, call the district attorney who prosecuted the case and interview her, suggests Connie Fletcher writing in *The Quill*. Especially when writing about celebrities, who tend to have prepared messages for every interview, Fletcher suggests doing crucial preliminary reporting by checking:

- The *Who's Who* directory to find "long-forgotten or long-hidden" information.
- An autobiography the celebrity wrote. "Here is the purest form of what the celebrity wants to talk about and the easiest way for you to find out what's important to the celebrity."
- *Biography Digest* to find any extensive articles done on your subject.
- Press releases.

What happens if you only have a few hours to prepare? "Don't make the mistake of assuming the celebrity will understand how busy reporters are, and will therefore be forgiving. Most people only understand how busy themselves are," Fletcher writes.

Often, you have to do a lot of pre-interviews on the phone to find the right people to showcase in your story. Let's say you get a tip that most of the football players at an expensive private college come from poor families. Because of various collegiate rules and regulations, players are unable to receive athletic scholarships. Consequently, many players attend the college during the fall semester, returning to community college in the spring. During the fall semester, they struggle to keep up academically, receiving poor marks, while they hold down two or three jobs to pay tuition.

You need to find out everything you can about the rules and regulations that prevent the players from getting scholarships. You need to find out from university officials what is being done to assist the players with finances and academics. Then you need to talk to as many players as possible, maybe without taking a single note, until you find the two or three who best exemplify the focus of your story: that many on the football team struggle to keep up academically and financially, while the university does little to assist them. The story should focus on the players, their obstacles and their struggles, with responses from university officials and experts who can explain if the practice is common and why.

That's a lot of interviews. You'll save yourself an enormous amount of wasted time if you make an interview plan: Whom will you interview first? What do you hope to learn? Ditto for your second interview, and third and so on. Save time by doing background interviews over the phone.

Become a Trained Observer

Begin taking notes—mental or written if possible—as soon as you're on your way to the interview. Look for telling details that illuminate the story's focus and your source's personality and character. What does the neighborhood where your source lives look like? When you visit the professor who just won the university's highest award for research, is her office so cluttered there's no space to put down a cup of coffee?

The New Yorker is one of America's premier general interest magazines, well known for the literary quality of its fiction and nonfiction. In a profile of John Adams, one of America's most vital and eloquent composers, writer Alex Ross uses telling details—observed during the interview—to illuminate Adam's character:

> At the age of 53, (Adams) has a youthful and friendly face, framed by a neat silvery beard. His eyes are sometimes bright with curiosity, sometimes clouded by a slight sadness. He loves to read, and his favorite gambit in conversation is to mention a book, such as the Ginsberg collection, that has excited him. If you saw him in Berkeley, where he lives most of the year, you might peg him as a U.Cal. professor—one of those plaid shirt intellectuals who sit outside the Cheese Board, on Shattuck Avenue, eating organic pizza and annotating Wittgenstein.

Teaching yourself to become a trained observer is much harder than you might imagine, warns feature writer David Fryxell, in *Writer's Digest*. "Most of the time I snooze through my surroundings just like most people. When I'm 'off duty,' the particulars of the world too often pass me by unnoted and unremembered." Fryxell is not alone, he adds. "Most of us let the torrent of information our senses collect leak away almost as fast as it hits our brains." That's why journalists have to train themselves to observe telling details. For the journalist, "retaining meaningful details from the everyday sensory overload can spell the difference between an ordinary piece of reporting and a story that comes alive for readers," Fryxell says.

So now the interview becomes even more challenging. Not only are you charged with asking the right questions and writing the responses accurately in your notebook, you also have to begin mentally searching your surroundings—and your source—for telling details as well. Fryxell offers a few tips to help make it easier:

- Let your eyes wander about the room, even as you keep most of your attention focused on the interview. Most sources "say some boring irrelevant stuff," he adds, allowing you time to look for details. "When your subject wanders off into an anecdote about his pet gerbil, continue to gaze at your subject and nod encouragingly," while noting details of his personality and surroundings. "Do his eyebrows twitch like frenzied caterpillars when he talks? Anything sticking out of his shirt pocket? Is his voice deep, wheezing, resonant? Does a clock on the wall of a high-powered executive ticktock relentlessly, like a metronome for his pressure packed career? Do the floors of the manufacturing magnate's office tremble with the distant pulse of the factory floor? Does the home smell of freshly baked bread, the production plant of ozone, the farm of recently spread manure?" Put your impressions down in your notebook.
- Show, don't tell. "Your subject might talk tough, say, but mentioning the 'Hang in there' kitten poster on his wall can round out your portrait. You could describe someone as 'nervous,' but it's far better to describe his constant pencil-chewing," says Fryxell.

Start your interview with a well-thought-out question. Feature writer Sheila Feeney was assigned a profile of actor Sean Hayes, best known for his portrayal of the over-the-top gay character Jack on the television comedy "Will and Grace." Before the interview, Hayes' publicist warned Feeney not to ask the actor about his sexuality. The first question Feeney asked Hayes: "I was told not to ask you about your sexuality. Why?"

For Feeney, control is a big issue. Most celebrities only do interviews when they have a movie or TV show to publicize. That's when they do publicity junkets, usually allowing each journalist a 15-minute interview in a hotel suite. Media trainers coach most famous people, training them to deflect questions and respond with a message track, "the stuff they want you to print," Feeney explains. When someone tells Feeney what not to ask, it only piques her curiosity. "When they make it a taboo, it's like they're trying to tell you, 'Don't talk about the elephant in the middle of the room. . .' " Public figures and officials "have to be able to handle any question lobbed their way. No one can tell you what you can ask or not ask. Stars can control what gets in the story by what they say in the 15 minutes they have with you."

Whether you're interviewing a celebrity or a nuclear physicist, anytime a source "says something important, ask a key question: 'How do you know that?' " says investigative reporter Eric Nalder. The question "sheds light on credibility, extracts more detail and is a door-opener to other sources. Also, ask people why they do what they do, rather than just asking what they do."

Profiles

While profiles focus most of their attention on a particular person, that doesn't mean yours should be a one-source story. All the same rules of interviewing and source-finding previously discussed apply here. "Seventy-five percent of your work should be done before you begin the interview," says Feeney. When Feeney begins work on a profile, she follows a simple rule: "Background ruthlessly," she says. Talk to people around your subject, their co-workers, enemies, mothers, fathers, children, grade school teachers. As the author of a profile, you draw on the tools of fiction writers. You want to draw your subject precisely, illuminating character and setting within a well-drawn, tension-filled narrative. That requires a lot of work, first in preparing for—then during—the interview.

To get the most out of the time you have with your source, organize the interview chronologically. Begin by asking questions about what life was like before the news event that brought you to him or her. Then arrange the interview's dramatic structure using the same formula Hollywood moviemakers use to create story lines:

- Life is normal—the status quo prevails.
- A disruptive event changes the status quo.
- The protagonist faces the problem and struggles to solve it.
- The character makes several wrong decisions, leading to a moment of despair, when solving the problem seems hopeless.
- The character discovers an insight or learns something new that leads to a solution.
- The status quo is remade.

The Importance of Character, Setting, and Plot

How do you mine the depths of character, setting, and plot to create a good profile? It's not as hard as you might think, but it may take some time. At the very least, make sure you a have a conversation in a place that's important to your subject. In his famous piece *Travels in Georgia*, writer John McPhee traveled around the state with two naturalists, documenting the decline of rural America and the march of the bulldozers. In a profile of "Who Wants to Be a Millionaire?" host Regis Philburn, author Elizabeth Colbert puts on exercise clothes and goes to the gym with him. If you're doing a profile of a place kicker, for instance, interview him or her on the football field during practice, kicking one ball after another. Ask questions that help you understand why someone would chose to spend hour after hour, day after day, week after week, month after month, kicking a football.

Go where the source takes you. *St. Petersburg Times'* writing coach Roy Peter Clark offers other tips for getting the most from sources:

- Come early and stay late.
- Start to interview before you take out the notebook and keep interviewing after you put it away. Some people tell you the most important thing after the recorder is off and the notebook is put away. As soon as you leave your source, write down what you've heard; rush back to your car or the bathroom and write it on your pants or your palms. Just get it down, Clark says. "You're not necessarily going to get exact quotes, but you'll get enough to paraphrase," he says.
- Never use interviewing as a substitute for direct observation. Try to observe your source engaged in dialogue

with another person; it's likely to be more illuminating than having him or her "spouting sound bites at you."

- Talk less. "I hate to listen to myself on a tape recorder doing interviews," Clark says. "I end up yelling 'Shut up!' at myself when I play back the tape."

- Silence is your friend. Wait for sources to fill the silence. Be patient. Repeat the question. Give people a chance to think.

- Don't just write down what sources say. Write down what you see. Body language. How they're breathing. What their hands are doing. What's on the wall behind them. Ask yourself: If you were doing an interview for TV, where would the camera be pointed? Then observe those details. Those are the telling details. If you're unsure about the story's focus, record details that interest you. Eventually you'll find the story's focus in the details.

- Invite your subject to take you on a tour. You might ask the source: "Would you mind showing me your collection of teddy bears? Do you have photos of the family? May I take a peak at your books? Wow that's a great old typewriter. How old is it?" When people take you on a tour they exemplify their values.

Control the Interview's Direction

Once you're conducting the interview, you need to control its direction. Interviewing expert John Sawatsky suggests imagining yourself as an explorer in control of a joystick that allows you to enter your source's brain, mine for information, and leave. You have a time limit, though, and like the computer game "Myst," the journey is filled with dead ends and wrong turns. If you ask random questions in no particular order, you'll never move forward quickly enough to reach your goal—what you believe is the story's focus—before your source's brain shuts down.

To help wend your way through the minefields, Sawatsky offers the following suggestions. First off, set your joystick to three positions only: Forward, On/Off, and Expand/Advance.

- Forward: Move forward chronologically. Avoid U-turns. "We can't reach our goal if we're going backwards," explains Sawatsky.
- On/Off: Classify each new assertion or revelation the source provides: Is it important? Incidental? Irrelevant? If sources take you on a tangent, off the path toward your goal, use your next question to put them back where you want them. If you suspect the tangent is more interesting than the goal, change your goal during the interview and follow that as your new path. If you're not sure what to do with tangential or incidental information, jot it down at the end of your notebook, or in a separate notebook, and ask about it at the end of the interview. Don't get distracted—or distract your source—with information that doesn't advance your goal.
- Expand/Advance: As you move forward through the chronology, you'll often want to stop and get a more detailed view or a close-up of the source's character or the story's plot. To illuminate the source's character, ask: What went through your mind? To advance the story's narrative or plot, ask: What did you do next?

When you're satisfied you've plumbed the depths of that particular plot point or explored as fully as you need the source's character trait, you advance or move forward.

The Question and Answer (Q&A) Format

Q&As look simple, but they're deceptively difficult. Always consult first with your editor before deciding to do a Q&A. "With Q&As, as with all dealings with your editors, the rule remains: No surprises," says author David Fryxell in *Writer's Digest.* You usually attempt Q&As in two cases: if you're reporting on a celebrity; or, if you're writing about a complicated subject, a self-help or how-to story, you might consider doing a Q&A—sometimes as a sidebar to the main story—to distill the main facts in an easy-to-digest format.

For a self-help, how-to, or technical story, the Q&A might not come from a single interview, but from information gathered from research and multiple interviews. "You are freed to answer readers' questions in the most straightforward manner," Fryxell explains, "without the complications of a lead, transitions, chronology." But, he warns, "by stripping your approach down to a Q&A, you toss away all the other tools at your command as a writer: description, narrative, characterization, conflict, contrast."

Sometimes, as with celebrity Q&As, readers are willing to forgo the literary niceties to hear as much as possible from the star. When reading a Q&A, people think they're "listening in on a single, uninterrupted and unedited conversation," says Fryxell. Wrong. "The transcripts go through a tremendous amount of processing, distillation and orchestration before publication." He refers to it as "squeezing the water" out of an interview. That means editing out the boring and repetitive stretches, "to extract and organize the essence of the conversation into a publishable manuscript." Remember, though, "if your subject can barely speak in coherent sentences, doesn't have much to say, or otherwise supplies answers that would make dull and painful reading, don't turn that torture into the As of a Q&A." (See Sidebar 7.1.)

Sidebar 7.1 Tales from the Street: Celebrity Manipulation
By Matt Coker, OC Weekly

I don't know about anyone else, but I popped open a bottle of champagne when Planet Hollywood shut its doors. What an over-hyped nightmare. I went to the opening and perhaps the first four "events"—usually some actor donating an article of clothing he or she wore in a movie. I believe the last time I went, Patrick Swayze gave them his shoes from "Dirty Dancing." Besides the screaming headaches I'd have after enduring all the fan shrieking and paparazzi flashbulbs, the last straw for me was learning that these "events" were carefully planned to happen once a month. Why? Because Planet Hollywood refused to advertise. We in the media were played like fiddles into showing up and providing them free advertising. It's not like they treated the press well, either. They would hound you with phone calls to come over, and when you got there you had to stay in a roped-off area. There was no actual interaction with the celebrity, unless you had a microphone and film crew with you. Then you got a 30-second sound bite.

A couple years ago, a local kid was starring with Arnold Schwarzenegger in "Last Action Hero." I was going to do a cover story, along the lines of, "local kid becomes huge star." We had his home number because we'd done stories before when the kid was in a famous Circuit City commercial. His dad said no problem to an interview, but he kept putting us off and putting us off. Then we'd get the kid's mother, and she seemed real sour on the thing, so we'd go back to the dad and he'd say he'd help us. But nothing happened. The story on the kid was slated to run in a week and we had bupkiss. Meanwhile, other interviews with this kid started popping up in the entertainment press. I tried to get in on the marathon interviews going on at some hotel in LA, but we were too low in the pecking order.

We'd just about given up when Planet Hollywood called and asked if we wanted to attend a premiere party with Arnold and the kid. I agreed to attend if the Planet Hollywood rep could get me a few minutes with the kid. No problem, she said. I pretty much ignored all the noisy and flashy hoopla because I was there for one reason: to get five minutes with this kid for our cover story, which had to be done the next day.

The kid was placed at a table next to his mom, and certain members of the media were taken to the table for their five minutes, including our photographer who snapped a quick shot for our cover. While I was sitting there, the Planet Hollywood person told me that I was going to get special access. After he was done in the restaurant, they would bring him back to me outside on the patio. "Go get a seat out there and I'll bring him to you in five minutes," she said. Instead of five minutes, she came back in 20 minutes. The kid is very tired, she said, but I could talk with him in 15 more minutes. So I waited. The woman came back and told me the mom decided he'd done enough interviews in the last two days. Sorry.

"But we're the hometown paper!" I yelled. Try the coconut shrimp, I was advised. I went back to work the next day, and told my tale of woe to my editor. "That's a great story," he said. "Run it." It seemed kinda whiny to me, but I did. The headline "Last Action Zero" ran over the kid's picture on the cover.

The mother got mad. The Planet Hollywood people got mad, even though I went to great lengths in the story to say how they had tried to help me out. Go figure.

A year or so later, a different PR guy invited me to lunch with a restaurant owner who was a partner in Planet Hollywood. When the owner—who some alleged had mob ties—found out what paper I was from, he cursed for five minutes the "Last Action Zero" story. I told him I'd pass his comments along to the writer.

8

Strategic Interviews

One of the biggest problems young reporters face is a lack of access. Sources never call back. They decline to be interviewed. They refuse to answer questions. Mike McGraw, the reporting coach at the *Kansas City Star,* says the reporters at his paper often complain, "It's as much work getting somebody to let me in the door as it is to get information out of them. And it's getting harder and harder."

In his long career as an investigative reporter, McGraw has developed a successful strategy to convince sources to grant an interview. When someone refuses to talk to him, he refuses to take no for an answer. He sends his biography and stories he has written to the recalcitrant source; he provides the source with references. He offers to buy lunch. "I'll tell them 'Let me tell you what I'm doing. I promise I won't ask a single question. And I'll pick up the tab.' "

Persistence is key, he says. "You've got to convince people you're not going to disappear tomorrow. A lot of people have the attitude: 'You don't care about me.' I tell my sources: 'I'm going to call back after the story runs. Tell me what you thought of it.'"

started talking. "I didn't take out a notebook; I just got him talking." During the conversation, he told Stanton, "I'd be a character witness for Pete Rose anytime." "Bill was in the car," Stanton recalls, "writing it all down."

If the source tries to deliver a message track or a "no comment," Stanton tries to get the source "on the team, that's one of my editor's favorite sayings. You want them talking to you. That doesn't happen over night, especially if they want to keep something under wraps or if the information you're after is highly sensitive." One strategy he and others suggest: Keep going back. Once, when Stanton was covering a federal corruption probe of city hall, he visited the home of a 70-year-old former convict who was under investigation. "We talked through the screen door for about 30 seconds; as soon as he saw the photographer, he slammed the door shut," Stanton says. That didn't stop Stanton. He returned to the office, called the source back, apologized for the photographer, and managed to keep him talking for 15 minutes. "He won't necessarily confess," says Stanton. "But you'll get good color and detail, and get him to confirm facts from other sources."

In certain cases, Stanton suggests "going for the surprise interview. Sometimes we like to surprise them so they don't have time to cook up an explanation." Once, Stanton had a tip that the mayor was using campaign funds to pay for his grandkids' birthday parties. When Stanton checked public documents, he saw the mayor had listed Dano the Clown as the entertainer at a political fundraiser. "We knew it was a birthday party, so we went to Dano the Clown's house. Dano was pulling out of his driveway, so we followed him to Dunkin' Donuts." Stanton and his colleague went on one side of the drive-through window just as Dano was pulling up to the other side. They started chatting, and wound up having coffee. "We started asking him questions. At first he was like, 'Oh yeah, sure I worked the mayor's grandkid's birthday party.' And he tells us he's never done any political fundraisers. Then it begins to dawn on him— Is this going to be a good story? Well, we say, that depends on your point of view. You've done nothing wrong."

"Then we go to the mayor's events coordinator, the one who booked Dano, and tell her we want to talk to her about events she planned for the mayor. She was fine with that, it's her job, right? So we ask her: Did you ever do anything personal for him? She says, 'Oh no! That would be illegal.' "

"So we whip out a bunch of documents that says otherwise: that she bought Christmas presents, wrote memos and letters on city stationary booking Dano the Clown for personal events, showed her signature on credit card receipts. So she says, 'I don't know how to explain that.' "

That was all they needed for an explosive story.

In another instance, Stanton and Malinowski were pursuing a particularly sensitive and controversial story. A white police officer had mistaken a black off-duty cop for a criminal, shooting and killing him. Stanton and Malinowski wanted to interview the white officer. They tried their usual strategy of talking to people around the white officer, urging them to persuade the officer to grant the interview. But those people were "telling him not to talk," Malinowski recalls. Malinowski appealed directly to the officer's attorney. "We told him (the officer) was being demonized by lot of people in Rhode Island, especially in the minority community. It's easier to demonize someone if you can't put a face on them or hear them respond. (He) looks like a cold-blooded killer. If we can show his human side, people will view him differently. It was the truth—of course we wanted to get the interview—but we told him the truth. That (he) looked like a white supremacist."

They got the interview.

Some other strategies Malinowski offers:

1. Get your sources to regard you as a sympathetic ear. "The biggest problem I see young reporters make is that they have 10 questions and they want to ask those 10 questions. Why would anyone open up to you if you're firing off 10 questions? Don't rush the process."
2. Go there. "It's easier to hang up the phone than it is to slam the door. See what's in their home or office."
3. Be disarming. "You can get a lot more information by being disarming than you can by telling someone they have to give it to you."
4. Be interested. People like to talk about what they do.
5. Develop criminal sources. They don't have a lot of people to talk to, they're bitter and they know how the system works.

A lot of times you only get one shot at interviewing your source, Stanton says. Be strategic: Interview junior people first to find out what they know, then go up the ladder. As you interview, ask yourself if the statements you're gathering are consistent or contradictory; if they're contradictory use that as the basis for subsequent lines of inquiry.

When you know you have to ask a tough question, blame it on someone else, suggests journalist and author Carol Rich: "Your opponent says you cheated on your income taxes. How would you respond to that?"

Remember, too, says reporter Eric Nalder, sometimes you have to "play it like you know. Ask the official 'why' he fired the whistleblower rather than 'if' he did. The question presumes you already know even if you don't have it confirmed. They'll start explaining rather than denying." It also never hurts, Nalder adds, to play the "lost reporter" role. "Say you need the person's help. 'Who is going to explain this to me if you don't?' "

Nalder has a strategy for "getting the confession," he says. Ask the source "for the names of people who support him or her. Then ask for the names of people who would criticize. Then ask what those critics are likely to say. This will jar loose uncomfortable information and tips. Ask whether the person has ever been disciplined or fired on the job or in school, charged with or convicted of a crime, arrested for drunk driving, sued or testified in court. Since all this stuff is on a record somewhere, people are reluctant to lie about it."

Whenever sources express an opinion or cite a fact, Nalder asks: "How do you know that?" "It's a great question for testing credibility," Nalder explains. "But it's also a fabulous doorway. If they answer the question: I heard it from Joe Blow, or I saw it in this or that document, or I was there, you've got an important piece of information. You can talk to Joe Blow. You can try to get the document." Nalder follows up with "How else do you know this?" "Every question should be followed up by 'How else?' That's how you hear about his brother. The other document." You also have to always ask "Why?" Nalder adds. "If we don't ask why, we will not be able to explain why. These questions may seem obvious to you. They are not. You need to train yourself to ask them."

When Nalder gets to the end of the interview, he shuts his notebook and reinterviews the source. "That's often when you get the best stuff. People will tell you a lot. Don't be dishonest and run out and put it in the paper. I will write it down and call back and get it on the record."

Before a story runs, Nalder calls back the key sources in his story and tells them everything he's going to publish. "I've gotten great quotes that way. It also builds a connection with them."

Putting P.R. People to Work for You

Nalder puts public relations people to work for him. "Respectfully, I give them assignments." For a story about an inadequate number of lifeboats on ferries, Nalder called the ferry company's safety officer. The safety officer told him "the records told how many lifeboats are on a boat." Nalder asked: "Where are the records?" He said: "In so and so's office." Nalder said: "Where?" He said: "In such and such filing cabinet." Nalder said: "What drawer?" He said: "The top drawer." When Nalder called the public relations person to ask for the records, she told him: "I'll have to get back to you. I don't know where they are." And Nalder said: "Well, they're in the top drawer of the such and such filing cabinet in so and so's office."

How to Keep People Talking When They Want to Quit

"That's enough," your source tells you. "I've run out of time." But you still have lots more information to get. Now what? The *Kansas City Star's* McGraw uses a couple strategies to keep his sources talking. First, he'll say: "You've given me enough information to be dangerous to myself and others. If I don't figure this out, readers won't understand the complexity of the issue. When can I see you again?"

If the source continues to refuse more time, McGraw says, "OK, but don't call me complaining when the story comes out." Some sources will say: "It's your job to get it right, not my job to make sure you get it right." That being the case, McGraw will "interview other people who can provide the information."

What do you do if sources become testy, hostile, violent, uncooperative or just plain shut up during the interview? A student reporter found out the hard way during a press conference featuring moviemaker Spike Lee. At the time, Lee had appeared in a commercial endorsing the fast food company Taco Bell; one of the students asked him a question about it. In response, Lee exploded and stomped off, abruptly ending the session.

Here's the exchange, published in a Northwestern University Medill School of Journalism newsletter:

> **Student:** "A friend and I were talking last night, and I don't know how true this is, but he was saying that black Americans are twice as likely to get heart disease as other segments of the population. In light of that fact, how do you justify lending your image to a company such as Taco Bell?"
>
> **Lee:** "How did (the) f—ing Rolling Stones get f—ing Budweiser to sponsor their f—ing tour? People die on the f—ing highways from drunk driving. What kind of f—ing question is that? This f—ing double standard.

Motherf—ing white performers, white entertainers, can endorse any f—ing product in the world . . . And I have to bear the f—ing weight of the whole race? 'Spike, how could you, in all your big consciousness, endorse a product like Taco Bell, when you know black people have, what, heart disease?' That's f—ing bulls—t, man. What kind of f—ing question is that? Would you ask f—ing Mick Jagger that? Why f—ing Budweiser is sponsoring their tour?"

What did the student do wrong? First of all, the reporter should have nailed down the evidence. Attributing a statistic to a friend who has no particular expertise in the subject, and then admitting that you're not sure if it's true, makes you look like an idiot. If the statistic is false, the question is unfair. If the statistic is true, how true is it? Make sure the evidence you gather is accurate. Questions are precise instruments, not blunt objects with which to cudgel unsuspecting sources.

Many times sources will intentionally try to intimidate or mislead you, regardless of how smart or prepared you are. When this happens to him, the *Star's* McGraw says he does the mental equivalent of whistling a happy tune. "Whenever you feel intimidated or fearful, think of your source in tattered clothes or in any environment that makes him or her more like you," McGraw says. He also reminds himself of his public duty. "I tell myself I represent people who want—and have the right—to know this information. If I allow this guy to intimidate me, I'm not working as hard as I should for my readers."

Sometimes sources will only allow you to interview them "off the record" or "on background." Double check with your source to make sure you and she agree on the definitions of these commonly misused phrases. "Off the record" means nothing said can be published in your story. "On background" means the information can be published, but not attributed to a named source. Many newspapers refuse to allow reporters to attribute facts, figures, and opinions to unnamed sources, so you'd better check your publication's policies before you write the story. If sources give you off-the-record information, ask them who else would know or what document will confirm what they've told you.

Making Sense of Nonsense

Listening to sources but not really understanding what they're saying is another problem reporters often face. Sometimes the reason is as simple as a reporter failing to do the appropriate homework before the interview or failing to pay attention during it. But sometimes sources like to confuse reporters with a well-worn trick: phrasing answers in the bloated jargon of their profession. This is especially true of computer company officials, financial bureaucrats, and anyone in the education profession. Never let a source erode your confidence. Simply ask for answers in plain English. Some will dodge direct questions with such a flourish you won't realize you don't have the answer until you're writing the story.

It is always the reporter's responsibility to understand fully what the source is trying to say. If you don't understand, you'll never write a coherent story or answer any of your editors' or readers' questions. Once, a student reporter turned in a story about the launch of a new campus program beset with problems. The student was assigned to find out how much money had been spent on the program and why the administration had failed to fix the problems. She returned with a confused muddle of a story that she intended to publish without revision. When her editor began asking her questions about comments made by one of her sources, the reporter responded: "I don't really know what he was trying to say. He was really confusing." The reporter failed to accomplish her most basic task: to understand a problem and to explain it clearly to readers or viewers.

Colombo and the Bureaucrats

Anyone who has ever spent any time at all trying to get something from government clerks knows how difficult even a most simple and reasonable request can be, especially if the clerk doesn't feel like working when you call or approach the window. Investigative reporter Don Ray has come to expect clerks will refuse to give him information he knows is public record. When that happens, he never pounds his fist on the counter, invoking the public's right to know. Instead, he adopts what he calls the Colombo strategy, named after the fictional television detective. He tells the clerk: "Oh, it's not public? That's great! I didn't want to work today anyway." He starts to walk away, stops, touches his forehead and says, "Oh, one more thing. My boss is gonna want to know why I came back empty-handed. Could you jot down the law or rule that explains why I can't have it?"

"Then they of course say they don't know. So I say: 'Would you mind letting me talk to somebody who might have the answer?' Then they get this guy and that guy and that guy until they finally bring up somebody who hasn't been to the window in a year, and he says, 'Oh yeah, that's public record.' And the clerk is really impressed with how you've bested the supervisor."

To avoid having to go through that routine every time, Ray gets friendly with bureaucrats. He makes an effort to know their names. He looks around their cubicles, observes their pictures and mementos, and uses his observations to establish rapport. If he sees photos of kids playing soccer, he might say, "Oh, my kid plays soccer," to get a friendly conversation going. He jots down a few personal things about the clerk in his notebook. Then when he returns in need of a favor, he always begins the conversation by greeting the clerk by name and asking a personal question: "How's the soccer team going?"

If you're calling and the clerk answers the phone with a personal greeting, for example, "This is William," respond with: "Hi William, how you doing?" "Talk to them like you know them. And they'll think, 'He knows me.'" That familiarity often predisposes them to help you. After you've established a personal rapport, ask the clerk for what you need. If it's a document, for example, and you really need the clerk to give you the information over the phone—which most will refuse to do—begin by saying, "I could drive all the way out there, but gosh, would you mind telling me who the attorney is?" Follow that up with, "Would you mind telling me who the plaintiff is?" Pretty soon, they're reading you the whole file.

Clerks and bureaucrats tend to be tight lipped with reporters, sometimes because they fear losing their jobs.

Let's say you've asked the question: "We're looking into problems in the purchasing department" and the source responds: "I couldn't talk to you about that." "Couldn't" often means "would like to but can't." Try another strategy, he suggests. Ask the bureaucrat: "If you were looking into this story, where would you go next?" The source might answer: "I'd talk to the guy who got fired last week or the guy who got the contract last week." You're on your way.

In one instance, Ray, who works in California, needed information from a marriage certificate in Michigan. When he called the government agency holding the certificate, the clerk told him she'd mail it tomorrow. Ray needed the information that same day. He asked her to read it to him. She said no. He tried every possible way to get what he needed. She refused to help him. Finally, he asked her: "Has anyone else ever found a creative way to solve this problem?" "Yes," she replied. "One man paid us extra to have it sent Federal Express." "Federal Express arrives the next day. How did he get it on the same day?" Ray asked her. "He called the Federal Express driver and had him read it over the phone." And that's what Ray did.

Taping and Note-Taking

A tape recorder is a useful tool that ensures your quotes will be accurate and in context. But taping interviews poses particular problems. First off, sometimes reporters will use tape recorders as a crutch, an excuse to stop paying attention and stop taking notes during an interview. Ever tried to transcribe an hour-long interview? It takes about 2½ hours.

Multiply that by three sources and you've missed your 5 P.M. deadline. Worse, the more students rely on tape recorders, the easier it is to put off learning the crucial skill of note-taking, which is best mastered, like the rest of journalism, by practice.

Use a tape recorder as a backup to taking notes and paying attention. Most recorders have numbers that track where a particular part of the conversation is on the tape. When a source says something you know you'll want to quote, note the number and go back to it later. Always bring fresh batteries and a spare tape to the interview; you never know when the recorder will malfunction or the batteries will die.

Listening carefully and critically is crucial to getting the information you need in an interview. The first rule of note taking is don't write everything down. Understand what your sources are saying, figure out their bias, and collect the background information you need to write the story. Once you've done that, start thinking about what you'll need to support the story's focus. Develop your own shorthand, then use it consistently, so you're able to read your handwriting later on. Jot down sentences that sum up your source's perspective in a nutshell or a sound bite. Don't stop there, though. Jot down the telling details that illuminate your story's focus.

In a piece author David A. Fryxell wrote about an astrologer, he described her "as crisp and businesslike as her desk: dressed all in white, curly brown hair cut close to her long face, speech as regular and rapid as a machine gun."

He explains how that sentence came into being: "Her clothing I'd noted during one lull in the interview, her hair in another; her rapid-fire speech (making my note taking more challenging) in a third pause between quotable quotes. None of these details required much of a detour from regular note-taking and interviewing." During the interview, Fryxell scrawled into his notebook: "crisp, biz-like," and "dr all white" and "hair curly brn." The sentences he formed "after the interview, back at the keyboard."

Sometimes circumstances prevent note-taking, especially if you're doing a feature or a profile and spending a week or several days hanging out with your source. For a profile of interview expert John Sawatsky, one reporter spent days and days with her source, in cars, buses, and restaurants, during seminars, in hotel rooms. Sawatsky loves to walk, so they spent a lot of time talking while criss-crossing the streets of Toronto, where it was nearly impossible to take notes, dodge traffic, and conduct an interview simultaneously. Whenever it was impossible to take notes, the reporter returned to her hotel room, and wrote down as much as she could recall of the conversation and the scene. One of those street conversations became the lead for her profile of Sawatsky (See Sidebar 8.1).

Sidebar 8.1: The Question Man
By Susan Paterno *American Jouralism Review*

Best-selling author John Sawatsky, Canada's premiere investigative reporter and a foremost expert on interviewing, is taking me for a stroll down a busy Toronto street. We're coming from the Canadian Broadcasting Co., where Sawatsky has spent the last two days training veteran journalists to forget everything they know about interviewing—because it's all wrong. As I try to keep up—his strides are nearly double mine—dodge traffic and ask questions, he keeps deflecting. At some point I realize this walk is leading somewhere else besides back to the hotel, to an understanding, to an epiphany, to a moment of sheer terror.

I'm trying the tactics on Sawatsky that he has been teaching me since we started talking several weeks earlier; I remain skeptical about his rules: Never make a statement during an interview. Never ask a closed-ended question. Sound conversational, but never engage in conversation. The advice may be simple, but the execution is about as natural as walking on hot coals. It's hit and miss, hit and miss until finally I come up with a question that seems to catch both of us off guard: Me because I can't remember what the question is, and him because he seems to have revealed something he is now attempting to sidestep.

He has mentioned that there are holes in his methodology, and those holes are preventing him from getting started on his latest book on interviewing, number six after five nonfiction best sellers. To Sawatsky, holes are great-unanswered questions, a reluctant admission that after nearly a decade of inquiry, he still has some way to go in creating the definitive examination of the interview, journalism's fundamental tool.

Holes, huh? I think smugly. The master stumbles.

"What holes?" I ask, using an open-ended, neutral question beginning with "what" a tactic that only one hour earlier Sawatsky had said produces the best results. A direct hit, I think, but I follow with a misfire: "I didn't see any holes in what you did today." Ouch. I commit one of Sawatsky's deadly sins. I make a statement. The savvy source with something to hide uses an interviewer's statement as an exit ramp, an easy way out of a question. I try to recover. "Where are the holes?"

"Well, mostly the holes are in what we're doing tomorrow," he says. "There aren't too many holes in what we did today."

"But where are the holes in what we did today?" I repeat. He says nothing. I want to say more; the silence makes me uncomfortable. Sawatsky's eyes dart back and forth across the street, looking for a place to cross. Or maybe he's looking for an exit ramp. I want to give him one, because I like him and my natural inclination is to try to help out.

Uh oh. I'm doing exactly what he says gets journalists into trouble. I'm giving into my social instincts rather than remaining a disciplined gatherer of information. Am I losing control of the interview?

"I guess mostly the holes are in what we're doing tomorrow. You know, it's like when you write a book. The reader never sees the holes, only the author."

"So where *are* the holes?" the question may be neutral but my voice is demandingly subjective, almost hostile. The traffic roars; I strain to hear his response. No response. I want to qualify, to explain, to justify, to say *something,* but I resist, letting the traffic whiz by, the horns bleat, the wind rush between us. Finally, he speaks.

"See that?" He says pointing to the street we're now crossing. "That's Yonge Street. It's the longest street in Canada." He proceeds with a mini travelogue about Toronto. Forget it, I think. I'll drop it. He wins, I panic: How am I going to get him to answer the question? What am I doing wrong? How am I going to fix it?

Clearly, he's on to me. But it's not just my problem. In Sawatsky's view, it's a problem for all journalism: Savvy sources are on to all of us, spinning back, all heat and no light, precisely because "we're asking the wrong questions," he says. Under attack, journalists are conceding defeat to well-oiled propaganda machines without really understanding why they're losing. In the last decade media trainers have become such a growth industry "you can even find them among small businessmen in Newfoundland," Sawatsky says, teaching politicians and executives "how to run circles around journalists."

"It's a sophisticated battle for control," he says. Sawatsky contends the "message trackers are winning," thanks to journalists who too often rely on outdated, conventional approaches to interviewing. Sawatsky denounces standard interviewing techniques as "the old methodology," often characterized as a power struggle between interviewer and subject, as a battle of wills, a game to be won or lost.

Sawatsky changes the framework, taking the mystery out of what most journalists have always believed is a mystical, serendipitous experience, likened to "lovemaking" by reporter Claudia Dreifus in a recent book on interviewing. The conventional method represents an irrational belief "in magic," says Sawatsky. "If an interview goes well, then we say it's magic. But it's not magic. It happens for an understandable reason. It's rational. It's a skill. It's easy to teach someone skills."

Interviewing by E-mail

Interviewing by e-mail can be useful in certain circumstances. "In one sense it's canned quotes," explains reporter Lance Williams in an article on the pros and cons of e-mail interviewing. "On the other hand, though, it's pretty coherent thoughts." E-mail can prove an invaluable tool for reporters who want to get to the source without the usual barriers—"flacks and protective secretaries," explains Russell Frank writing in *The Quill*. "If nothing else, it saves time. Rather than hear, 'Mr. Jones is with somebody. May I ask what this is about?' you can get your question to

Mr. Jones without some intermediary deciding when and if to tell him a pesky reporter is on the phone."

E-mail also does the job well for reporters who need to get quick follow-up questions answered or facts confirmed. For instance, you might e-mail this question to a source as a follow-up: "You mentioned in our conversation that the conversion to morning production cost the company millions of dollars. How much did it cost exactly?" If in your source's response she fails to provide you with the dollar amount, you can e-mail back until your source has answered the question. E-mail also works well if you have an ongoing relationship with a source and you need a quick question answered.

"But as a technique for interviews," writes Frank in *The Quill*, "it's the pits." Generally, e-mail fails to do the job for reporters "on deadline, if you're looking for emotional reactions or opinions, if you're dealing with someone uncomfortable with technology, or if you have no way of verifying that the person who sent the e-mail is the person who wrote it."

Sidebar 8.2: Interviewing Made Easy By John Sawatsky

Interviewing expert John Sawatsky believes reporters could improve their interviewing skills markedly by following some strategies. Sawatsky offers the following suggestions:

1. **Ask neutral, open-ended questions.** Start questions with what, how, and why; they demand the most from sources, requiring them to describe causes (what happened?), processes (how did it happen?), and motivation (why did you do it?). Fill

in the blanks with questions beginning with who, where, and when. Beware the traps:

Trap 1: "How do you feel?"

If you ask a mother who has just lost a child or a worker whose factory just closed down or an athlete who just won a big game "How do you feel?" the question will almost always fail. Why? "They don't know how they feel. It's too soon for them to articulate how they feel," Sawatsky explains. Wait until the source has had ample time to reflect on what happened. Then, "the question works quite well."

Trap 2: The problem of counterbalancing:

Sources nearly always make up for a lack of neutrality by counterbalancing or counteracting, overblown questions with modest responses. In one example, Larry King tells John F. Kennedy Jr.: "You don't have a normal life."

> JFK Jr. responds: "I have a pretty normal life."
> King: "Is it hard being the son of a legend?"
> JFK Jr.: "No, it's not hard."

The source, Sawatsky says, "feels compelled to give arguments for the other side." King should have asked: "What's it like being the son of JFK?" and let Kennedy fill in the blank.

2. **The more a question huffs and puffs, the more it blows.** The more information journalists put into questions, the more information sources leave out. Less is more: Short questions produce succinct, dramatic, focused responses. Long rambling questions usually get long rambling answers or curt, confused responses.

3. **Open people up through strategy.** Strategy becomes especially important when the issue is difficult for the source. Ask

yourself: What's the goal? Then devise a strategy to achieve it. A reporter came to Sawatsky with a statistic she wanted to humanize: One-third of the school children in Edmonton, Canada, were going without breakfast. Asking children directly: "Did you eat breakfast this morning?" Would likely produce a less than truthful response since even small children are socialized to avoid admitting that they're hungry and poor. Ask instead a series of questions designed to get a truthful response: "What's the first thing you did when you got up this morning? Then what? Then what? Then what? Until the child arrived in school. If the child made no mention of breakfast, you ask: What about breakfast? Why didn't you eat anything? What happens to you when you don't eat breakfast?"

4. **Establish agreement.** The reporter and source must agree on basic facts. Without agreement, reporters spend most of the interview trying to force the source to accept their version of events, usually resorting to coercion and leading questions. When reporters had evidence that President Bill Clinton was having sex with an intern, they should have forced Clinton to agree to a definition of what constitutes sexual relations. Clinton was able to deny his dalliance precisely because he stubbornly refused to define what he did as "sexual relations."

5. **Build the interview on answers, not questions.** People find it easier to volunteer than to admit. When the source makes an original assertion, follow up with a question asking for evidence to support it.

6. **Put the burden of proof on the source.** To focus your questions, pick a key phrase you want to probe. Repeat it. Ask a what, how, or why question. If in describing his marriage, Ted Kennedy says, "We've had difficult times," respond: "What do you mean by difficult times?"

- Use the source's exact words. If you change the words even a little, the source no longer owns the statement.
- Stay in the moment. Sawatsky advises against dredging up old clips and asking a source to defend an illuminating revelation made months, weeks or even days earlier. "If you give sources time to think, they'll usually disown what they've said."
- Never repeat phrases in your question from a source's message track; it will always result in more message track.
- Make no original assertions in the interview. "We either require the source to provide the evidence to substantiate subjective statements, or we introduce our own values and subjectivity into the interview and risk being forced by a savvy source to prove ourselves and defend our statements," explains Sawatsky. A question beginning with "how" pushes sources to go further or exposes them, forcing them to respond. If a source, for instance, insists, "There was no crime," ask, "How do you know that?" If a source says, "I can't remember" ask, "Why can't you remember?"

9

The Ethical Interviewer

The First Amendment to the Constitution is a unique document that protects free speech and puts the press beyond government control. It also allows journalists to fabricate, betray sources, slant stories, and lie to their editors. But it is a tribute to American journalism that such practices are the exception, not the rule, and that journalists themselves are the main watchdog over unethical behavior of their colleagues. *Columbia Journalism Review, American Journalism Review,* and *Brill's Content* are among the publications that keep a weather eye on the transgressions of journalism. The Society of Professional Journalists, IRE, and the American Society of Newspaper Editors (ASNE) also stress strict ethical standards. The greatly improved alternative press, once an unruly group not known for its professionalism, also keeps a sharp eye on the ethics of the mainstream media as do various academic critics.

Reporters who have made up facts or whole stories have been fired and their careers ruined. Plagiarists have met the same fate. Journalists working for mainstream media, who regularly slip in their own biases and prejudices into their copy do not last long, the exception being columnists and editorial writers, who are generally free to vent their opinions. Objectivity is alive and well in the media despite the skeptics' belief that it doesn't exist. In recent years, news organizations and journalist groups like ASNE have engaged in deep soul-searching about their profession, urging that more emphasis be placed on fairness and accuracy.

In interviewing, the least the source expects from you is honesty—faithfully reporting his words as spoken and not attributing other words to him or using his words out of context with false and/or damaging results. Here are the ethical issues to be aware of in an interview.

Inventing Quotes—Don't

Some reporters don't think a source's comments are interesting enough so they make up others that will play better in print. The reporter may be right in seeking more lively or more relevant answers but it's unethical to supply them. The creative journalist, realizing she is dealing with an unproductive or hesitant source, comes up with more provocative questions to stimulate more provocative responses, or she challenges porous answers. Murray Teigh Bloom, author of best-sellers (*The Man Who Stole Portugal,* and others), suggests that writers frustrated by a dry interviewee develop "a lever of interest" that may be obtained from other sources who know the individual and may be a friend or enemy. Bloom also advises that, in opening an interview, the reporter should, "Keep the tape recorder and the notebook out of sight for the first ten minutes and just talk casually and vaguely to get the measure of the person and how high he or she scores for directness and evasion."

Manufactured quotes can lead to complaints from the subject, a reprimand—or worse—from an editor, and even a lawsuit against you and your publication. Of course, there are sources who deny their true statements after they see them in print. In this case, you may have to produce your notes or tape to confirm your accuracy. Some sources are so worried they'll be misquoted or misinterpreted that they ask to see the copy before publication. Most newspapers and reporters deny such requests, fearing that the subject will go beyond correcting facts to taking on the role of editor over the whole piece. Still, in certain types of articles—usually medical or scientific—writers for newspapers and magazines have allowed an interviewee to review the copy for factual mistakes only.

San Francisco Chronicle Science Editor David Perlman declines to provide his sources a copy of his story but will read back on the phone to him material he is putting in quotation marks or will summarize what he learned from the interview. Perlman says it's impractical to submit a copy to a source, "the time element being one reason. Another is that the story often deals with other areas besides the subject's own portion and that it may involve commentary or interpretation."

Your Words—His Words

While journalists overwhelmingly eschew the coining of quotes for lackluster subjects, there is less agreement on the practice of "cleaning up" quotes to correct grammar, eliminate profanity, or erase ethnic or racial slurs. A number of writers and their publications have no problem with doing a little surgery on bad grammar, editing out swear words, or eliminating personal or generic insults. In a recent survey of 271 journalists around the country by the Committee of Concerned Journalists, six in ten approved fixing grammatical mistakes such as switching "ain't" to "isn't" or having verbs and pronouns agree. According to a report of the study in the *Columbia Journalism Review,* "Many volunteered that this is acceptable because it adds clarity for the reader and corrects slips by the speaker."

But are they slips? In the span of a reporter's career, he will interview high-school dropouts as well as college graduates. It can be argued that dressing up the quotes of, say, a construction worker with an eighth-grade education, may take the flavor out of his hard-nosed comments, thus diluting a story about a labor dispute. Readers are better able to form a picture of the interviewee if he is served up "as is." Take, for example, a desert hermit whose speech is larded with colorful phrases, irreverent observations, and faulty grammar. You would lose the best part of the story by making him sound like an English teacher. However, there is a possibility that a hermit could be an English teacher himself or a rocket scientist in search of a different lifestyle. Interesting hermits have turned up.

Newspapers, magazines, and broadcast stations tread very gingerly when the quotes include racial or ethnic badmouthing. Often, the decision to leave them in or take them out depends on who is talking. In the case of known racists such as Ku Klux Klan leaders, who have become public figures, their diatribes, however distasteful, may stay because that is what defines them. On the other hand, a source who gratuitously—or unknowingly—maligns a group or individual may not see his actual words in type.

Printing or broadcasting profanity is usually a matter of the publication or station's policy. A "hell" or a "damn" will generally not be edited out, but in most of the mainstream press, the "f" word and the "s" word are taboo or will be represented by the first and last letters separated by dashes. Magazines also vary in policy. *Penthouse* and *The Ladies' Home Journal* do not generally target the same audience. Again though, the flavor of a story can be lost or diminished by sanitizing the person's speech. To make a Hells Angels biker sound like a banker could make a story laughable. Don't be afraid to argue the point with an editor, particularly if the publication is flexible about such references. You were there; the editor was not.

To sum up: although journalists may differ on such practices as adjusting grammar, changing words or phrases for clarity (not for meaning), or toning down profanity, there is virtually universal accord that an interviewee's published quotes must be his or her own—not the writer's. The Poynter Institute in St. Petersburg, Florida, which holds seminars for professionals on various aspects of journalism, developed "two overarching principles" for reporting, according to Roy Peter Clark, one of its officers: "Do not Add, Do Not Deceive." Writing in *Columbia Journalism Review,* Clark and Tom Rosenstiel of the Committee of Concerned Journalists elaborated: "In reconstructing quotes or events the journalist did not witness, avoiding addition or deception requires that the audience know what is being done, specifically and precisely where . . ."

The Balancing Act

In letting off steam, a subject can provide you with great copy. But if his fulminations include offensive remarks about other people you're faced with a legal and ethical obligation. The remarks could be libelous, which would bring close scrutiny by an editor and/or the publication's lawyer. Broadcasters, too, must be careful of what gets on the air. But even if there is no libel, fairness demands that a maligned person be given a chance to respond, if only to complain that his position was misrepresented. Political candidates say a lot of harsh things about their opponents in the heat of a campaign. But, in recent years, the policy of the mainstream media has been to provide readers and viewers with the "other side" of a controversy. In fact, there could be several sides.

If a political candidate or officeholder excoriates an opponent, the fair move on your part is to give the other individual an opportunity to respond. The same is true of interviews with people charged with crimes, blunders, or mismanagement. The operative word here is *charged*. They may or may not be culpable. But while the charges are being sorted out you have an ethical duty to balance out the story. In the historic Florida vote battle, the journalists' claim of neutrality and fairness was put to the test as perhaps never before.

Let's say, for instance, that a male elementary school teacher is charged with molesting girls in his class. Obviously, you would include his denials in your account, but go beyond that. Find out from colleagues and the principal anything you can about his past record at the school or at other schools. Talk to neighbors on his street to get their take on the man. Often in such cases, the suspect is regarded as a model citizen and teacher and his fellow instructors and neighbors are astounded at the accusations. It is not being suggested here that you become the man's defender or determine his guilt or innocence. That's for the authorities—and perhaps a jury—to decide. As a journalist, however, you should, in fairness, equalize the story as much as you can. The Code of Ethics of The Society of Professional Journalists states: "The news media should not communicate unofficial charges affecting reputation or moral character without giving the accused a chance to reply."

Fairness also extends to simple disagreements, especially if the public welfare is concerned. When Theodore A. Postol, prominent MIT physicist claimed that the Pentagon's proposed anti-missile system would not work and accused the Defense Department of covering up its shortcomings, newspapers printed his remarks. But not before they contacted Pentagon officials, who countered that Postol's opinion was based on irrelevant flight tests. TRW, the company that conducted the tests, also was asked for comment but declined. Only then was the story ready to be published. A similar case of standard journalistic fairness was demonstrated in a *New York Times* article in 2000, reporting that Special Counsel John C. Danforth's investigation had absolved federal agents from blame in the 1993 fire that killed about 80 people at the Branch Davidian compound in Waco, Texas. The newspaper also quoted the Branch Davidian's lawyer Michael Caddell, who charged that Danforth's report was flawed and vowed to continue his wrongful death lawsuit against the government.

The process can also work in reverse. In the course of an interview you may find it necessary and fair—as well as newsworthy—to relay to the source criticism directed at him or his position on a certain matter. If he wants to reply, take it down. If, in the course of replying, he disparages his critics anew, you might want to go back to the latter for their reaction. But, this round-robin must be cut off at some point or you'll never get your story written. The author recalls a newspaper colleague on the labor beat who spent so much time on the phone collecting charges and countercharges from union and management officials in connection with a strike that an exasperated editor finally shouted at him: "Either get to the writing stage now or own the best story on the spike." He meant that further delay would result in the piece not being published because of deadline demand.

While you're collecting quotes from various sources it is well to keep in mind the observation of Leslie Gelb, president of the Council on Foreign Relations, who states: "Journalists are not in the business of pretending that all sides tell the truth equally." Reporters strive for the truth but sometimes determining it can take too long.

Some journalists believe their colleagues have gone overboard in their zeal to balance an article with opposing voices. Of course, editorial writers and many columnists don't extend themselves to include "the other side" in their pieces but the above-mentioned journalists also feel that certain stories in the rest of the newspaper or magazine need not be draped with dueling quotes.

Writing in *Editor & Publisher* magazine, Alica Mundy declares: "There are some stories to which there is *no other side* to the story." She cites such examples as the Holocaust, the Japanese attack on Pearl Harbor, Pol Pot's murderous rampage in Cambodia and the Watergate revelations." (T)oo many attempts by naïve reporters to let people air their versions of the 'other side' is resulting in revisionist history that would make Stalin smile," she asserts.

Her point may be well taken but our advice is to very carefully choose the stories in which only one side is presented. The standard of mainstream American journalism is still based on fairness and balance. You may find a child killer's excuses abhorrent and absurd but they belong in your article. Let the reader, not you, be judgmental.

Keep Your Emotions out of It

After his speech at the University of Notre Dame, Ted Koppel, anchor and managing editor of ABC News' "Nightline," was asked from the audience: "What kind of impact do your emotions have on your interviews?" Replied Koppel: "It's not as difficult as you think. The day is 24 hours long and I'm free to express and vent my emotions for 23½ hours of the day. I'm supposed to try and be professional for a half hour a day."

Most journalists must be professional longer than a half hour, probably including Koppel in his off-air conversations with sources. But whatever the length of time, it's vital that a journalist not let his or her emotions affect the kind of questions asked, the way they are asked and the response to them. Don't sneer, register disbelief, argue against, or endorse any expressed viewpoint. Exceptions can be made for comments on the weather, the high price of gasoline, or any other subject that does not impinge on the thrust of the interview. In short, maintain your professionalism. Of course, reporters are not robots and are just as prone to strong feelings about issues and people as anyone else. But they are trained by education and experience to not allow their emotions to color an interview. A truly fair and objective journalist should be able to interview Mother Teresa and a convicted terrorist with equanimity. Indeed, terrorists are interviewed fairly frequently in various parts of the world, including Osama bin Laden, accused mastermind of attacks against American troops and property.

Off the Record

At some point in many interviews, the subject will ask if his next statement can be "off the record." He or she may be a high government official, Teamster organizer, or corporate whistle-blower whose job would be jeopardized if the information got out. If the reporter agrees to the request, he is, in effect, promising that neither the remarks nor their source will be published. The pact is governed by no law but experienced journalists know that violating it is a serious breach of ethics. Moreover, the source is not likely to ever trust the reporter again. And if word gets around in media circles that a confidence was broken, the interviewer's reputation will suffer among his colleagues in the belief that the profession itself has been sullied.

Most reporters will go along with the off-the-record appeal, although some adamantly refuse to hear anything they cannot print. A famous editor had a sign on his desk that said: "Tell me nothing in confidence." However, the prevailing opinion among journalists is that they have nothing to lose by respecting the request. If they refuse, they learn nothing. By granting it, they may pick up vital information that can be confirmed elsewhere. And there is always the chance that the speaker will change his mind later. It has happened. You might, for example, acquire information after the interview that, conveyed to your subject, may cause him to reconsider.

In some interviews, the subject, at the outset, may insist on ground rules that protect certain things he will say. This generally means that the reporter will stop taking notes and/or turn off his tape recorder when an off-the-record statement is made. A word of caution: don't suggest going off the record. Sources, who otherwise might be inclined to speak freely, may regard your suggestion as a great idea.

Deep Background

"Deep background" sessions are common in Washington, D.C., where top administration officials or Congressional leaders invite selected reporters to lunch, dinner, or an evening gathering to impart information that must remain under wraps. Some news organizations have refused to attend these sessions in the conviction that material that can't be printed is of no value to them. Other media organizations resent the fact that only certain reporters are invited to the meetings, suspecting that they represent news companies that have been favorable to the administration or to a particular politician.

The anointed, though, believe the gatherings offer an opportunity to know key sources more intimately and perhaps win their confidence. The day will come, they reason, when the officials will tip them off to a Page 1 story with no restrictions on content or identification.

"Print It, But Don't Use My Name"

In a *New York Times* story about a doctors' boycott of Merck & Company's pharmaceutical products, a "Merck official" is quoted on the effects of the boycott on the firm's sales force. A *U.S. News & World Report* article quotes a "U.S. official," who estimates that 90 percent of the police superintendents in a certain country are "tainted." The writer of a *New Yorker* piece delving into Hillary Clinton's campaign for the United States Senate was told by a "Democratic elected official" from New York City that she and her advisors "seem to have a tin ear for New York politics."

In each instance it is safe to say the writer would have preferred to use the name of his or her source. Identifying sources lends credibility to a story while anonymous figures could create suspicion that they were made up by lazy or incompetent reporters who didn't do their leg work. But in all probability the journalist did not have a choice if she wanted the statement. Virtually every reporter has encountered the source who agrees to be interviewed with the caveat that his remarks are not for attribution—"Don't name me." Their reasons vary. In the *Times* story, the Merck spokesperson may have been a company public relations representative who, as in many companies, remains anonymous in dealing with the media. The person quoted in the *U.S. News* article might have been a State Department official who wanted his identity shrouded for diplomatic reasons. The politician, who belittled Mrs. Clinton and her aides is, like her, a Democrat and perhaps did not want to be accused of disloyalty to the party or damaging her chances for election. Hillary Clinton is said to have a long memory.

In some instances jobs or careers may be jeopardized by allowing a reporter to name his source. A low-level government employee who tells of his boss' illegal activities is a good candidate for firing. It can get more serious. An informant's life may be on the line if his or her name becomes known. Hard news reporters often must depend on all kinds of people for information, including gang members, cops snitching on their corrupt fellow officers, ex-spies, and so on. Moreover, you can't afford to be judgmental about *why* a subject is willing to supply you with facts that may send someone to prison. The source may indeed be motivated by high ideals in wanting to end corruption or clean up a polluted lake. Or his motivating factor may be to even an old score with a superior or co-worker—in short, revenge. Your sole concern should be whether the information is true and if you can trust the source. More of this in a moment.

The most famous hidden source of the twentieth century was "Deep Throat," the main contact for Bob Woodward and Carl Bernstein in their legendary investigation of the Watergate break-in, which earned the *Washington Post* a Pulitzer Prize and drove thousands of college-bound men and women to select journalism as their major. To this day, neither Woodward and Bernstein nor their editors have revealed Deep Throat's name, although former *Post* executive editor Ben Bradlee said it will be made known when the source dies. Meanwhile, all sorts of speculation has arisen over the cloaked source. Some observers in the media and elsewhere have suggested that Deep Throat existed only in the minds of Woodward and Bernstein. Others have theorized that he was a composite of various sources in President Richard Nixon's administration, who fed the revelations to the pair. Still others have named who they believe was Deep Throat.

Various news organizations have their own policies for dealing with anonymous sources. The Associated Press uses them under strict guidelines for writers. The rules are:

- Fact only—no opinion
- Fact critical to the story
- Fact unattainable in any other fashion
- Fact verified whenever possible by a second source

The "whenever possible" inclusion takes into account that AP is a 24-hour, seven-day-a-week news service with clients all over the world. Time is of the essence. Still, AP will not move a story whose accuracy is in serious doubt. States AP managing editor Darrell Christian: "Whenever possible, we try to include as much information as we can about who those sources are or at least what their positions are relative to an investigation." When the wire service does move a false report—usually based on false information—it follows with a correction as soon as the mistake is uncovered.

Unnamed sources always have been a troubling issue for the news media. Reporters, editors, and the public prefer identified sources but also know that it is sometimes not possible to obtain them. Eyebrows were raised when the *Bakersfield Californian* published a Page 1 story about an alleged romantic relationship between a U.S. congressman and a health industry lobbyist, both of whom were married to other people. The paper, which used secondary, anonymous sources, was accused by the legislator's chief of staff of being "fed lies and repeating those lies." *Californian* executive editor Mike Jenner acknowledged in a letter to readers that even public officials are entitled to a degree of private life, but he pointed out that the congressman headed a health-care finance committee in Washington and that the relationship represented a possible conflict of interests. He termed the story a matter of "significant public concern." Jenner added that the *Californian* also unsuccessfully sought out sources who could dispel the liaison rumors.

In an *Editor & Publisher* magazine account of the controversy, Aly Colon, who teaches ethics at Poynter Institute, a newspaper study and training center, termed the *Californian*'s story an important one but one with built-in problems. "If you had names and can judge where sources are coming from, you could add or subtract from the validity of those comments," he observed. Readers, he went on, are left to ponder the extent of the relationship, which "muddies the waters" about a vital subject.

Your End of the Bargain

Woodward and Bernstein have adhered to an ethical tradition among professional journalists. They did not "burn" their source. As stated previously, the unwritten rule is that if you agree to accept information from a source on the promise that his identity will not be revealed, you must keep that promise. The conventional wisdom is that breaking the pledge will cut you off forever from that source and very likely from other sources as well because they won't trust you anymore. This would be particularly devastating to an investigative reporter who often relies on people who will talk only if they remain nameless.

But promising anonymity might not be solely up to you. With media libel suits on the rise, many editors are demand-

ing that reporters share their source's identity with them—
and perhaps the news company's attorney. Editors want to
be convinced that Mr., Mrs., or Ms. Anonymous is legitimate and truthful. Of course, there is no foolproof assurance of this but newsroom managers are more likely to let
the reporter's story run if the source happens to be a public official, corporate executive, police officer, or generally a
reputable citizen. Crime figures or known snitches are likely
to give editors second thoughts although they are used as
sources.

Bob Greene, former assistant managing editor of *News-
day* and now a journalism professor, once said at an Investigative Reporters & Editors' conference: "If a reporter
refuses to tell me the name of his source, I tell him that I
can refuse to publish his story and I won't." At times, however, a source turns to be someone with a less-than-clean
reputation—a con, ex-con, drug dealer, even a suspected
murderer. Reporters and editors must weigh his or her
background and veracity against what they contribute to
the story.

Editors also are prone to take out insurance on the validity of the material brought in by a reporter. *Washington Post*
editor Ben Bradlee ordered Woodward and Bernstein to
confirm Deep Throat's utterances with at least two other
sources, a practice that other editors insist on. In his autobiography, *A Good Life* (Simon & Schuster, 1995), Bradlee
comments on the juicy tips Deep Throat dished out to
Woodward and Bernstein, involving bugging phones, tail-
ing people, planting spies, false press leaks, fake letters, and
theft of documents, all allegedly ordered by White House
staffers or Republican party officials. Writes Bradlee: "Many
people wondered then—and even now, so many years

later—how the *Post* dared ride over the constant denials of the president of the United States, and the attorney general of the United States, and top presidential aides. . . . The answer isn't that complicated. Little by little, week by week, we *knew* our information was right when we heard it, right when we checked it once and right when we checked it again. . . ."

Who Is Using Whom?

Although reporters and editors may sometimes argue over the latter's right to know the source's name, both know that many whistle-blowers are serving their own agenda and will, if they can, manipulate news people for their own ends. This is a time-honored trade-off, not only with anonymous sources but in journalism generally. The reporter knows he is being used but is willing to play the game for the sake of a timely and important story. The *AP Log*, a publication of Associated Press, notes: "Officials speak to reporters on a not-for-attribution basis for a variety of reasons, not all of them altruistic. They want to give their views exposure. They want to float trial balloons. They want to sell reporters and readers on what they see as the indisputable logic of their behavior. Or they just consider the information they are giving too sensitive to put out on any other basis."

Yet, when a deal is made with a source, whatever his or her motives, the reporter is ethically bound to honor it unless released from the "contract." There have been cases in which the source, for one reason or another, has let a journalist off the hook. The basis for secrecy may have vanished or the information was echoed by a source who went on the record.

Barring that eventuality, a reporter should be prepared to risk jail to keep his or her word to a confidant. And jail is where several journalists have landed in recent years because they refused to divulge their sources. One of the most recent is Tim Crews, editor of the *Sacramento Valley Daily Mirror* in California, who balked in court at revealing his source for a story about a Highway Patrol officer accused of stealing a firearm. He spent five days behind bars. In a similar dilemma, J. Harry Jones, a court reporter for the *San Diego Union-Tribune,* decided, in the face of a judge's order, to release his unpublished notes from a jailhouse interview with a murder suspect. The alternative for Jones was a jail sentence. The notes, which had been requested by the attorney for the accused man, contained no confidential information, according to Jones.

The *Union-Tribune* fought the order all the way up to the California Supreme Court and lost. In a statement reported by the paper, Jones noted in connection with unpublished material: "We are seeing more and more of defense lawyers wanting the notes. It's very disturbing. It's unclear what the ramifications of the long term will be. If people are going to be hauled into court whenever they have interviewed a criminal defendant and have to incur the costs to fight these issues, I worry editors will say, 'don't even bother going for that interview.' We don't want to get into that position."

A reporter can be subpoenaed as a witness in a trial, put under oath, and asked to name his source. The demand can originate with either the prosecutor or a defense attorney. If a judge holds that the reporter's testimony is vital to one side or the other, he can declare the journalist in contempt with the threat of jail if he continues to insist on preserving his source's anonymity or he refuses to turn over his notes. TV stations face the same threat with their outtakes. For his stand, Crews received the James Madison Freedom of Information Award from the Northern California Chapter of the Society of Professional Journalists (SPJ).

Doug Underwood, a University of Washington journalism professor, was ordered by a Superior Court judge to turn over his notes for a *Columbia Journalism Review* article about 18 laid-off staffers at the *Arizona Republic* in Phoenix. Underwood appealed the order on the grounds that his notes did not involve confidential sources and were thus protected by the First Amendment. The Washington State Court of Appeals ruled in his favor.

Most states have "shield" laws designed to legally protect a journalist's confidential relations with his sources. Some of these laws have gaping loopholes that force a reporter to reveal information under oath. In other cases, a judge may decide that a defendant's right to a fair trial supersedes the shield statute.

Gag Orders

In high-profile trials, a judge may impose a "gag" order on lawyers, witnesses, jurors, and defendants in the case. The command prevents them from making any public statements concerning any part of the court's business, including pre-trial proceedings. The First Amendment protects the media in writing or broadcasting news of the case but the gag does make it much tougher to obtain critical interviews. Normally, reporters do not attempt to interview jurors during a trial (unless they have a desire to be cited for contempt of court) but lawyers and witnesses are standard sources of information. Attorneys for both sides are often approached during recesses and at the end of the court day for questions about strategy, future witnesses, or explanations of motions and rulings.

No orders are foolproof, however. Leaks happen. They may come from lawyers, an investigating police officer, witness, bailiffs, or from the defendant himself. When confronted with impediments from any source, journalists are trained to get news and they get it any way they can without breaking the law. They don't turn a deaf ear to someone who wants to tell them something on an anonymous basis. Judges, or course, are irate when the gag is violated and will deal harshly with violators—if they discover them. Gag orders also have been imposed on their underlings by prosecutors, mayors, city managers, police chiefs, and other officials. The latter do not have contempt power but they can fire, demote, or otherwise punish the culprits. During the so-called "Whitewater" investigation in the 1990s of former president Bill Clinton by then-independent counsel Kenneth W. Starr, there were several probes of alleged news leaks of grand jury material, supposedly emanating from Starr's office. One of his top aides, Charles G. Bakally III, was tried on criminal charges in connection with the leaks and found innocent. If cities were ranked on the number of leaks to the media, Washington would win hands down.

Paul Grondahl, a staff reporter for the Albany (New York) *Times Union,* had to be resourceful in gathering material for his shocking series, revealing that 5,700 state prisoners were being held in "extreme isolation," locked up in tiny cells for 23 hours a day for months and years. State correctional officials, according to Grondahl, "refused to supply even basic facts, including the names of special prisoners in special units. Many of these prisoners are isolated in distant reaches of the state. Access by the press and prison watchdog groups is generally blocked."

So the reporter bypassed official channels to get the story. To obtain essential interviews with inmates, Grondahl resorted to weeks of clandestine correspondence with convicts and face-to-face meetings with them in prisons. "What I did was visit family members and get enough information so I could go to a facility with enough information to convince authorities there that I was a friend of the family," he recalls. The result was first-hand accounts that officials tried to suppress. The *Times Union* noted that inmates spoke up despite their knowledge that they could be punished.

To repeat: A good reporter overcomes obstacles to get the story. Be imaginative.

Whether dealing with a gag order or recalcitrant officials, cultivate sources who may be willing to spill out information despite a roadblock. They may have self-serving reasons for doing so or genuinely believe that disclosure is in the public interest, but motivation is generally not your concern.

The Spinning Wheel—Twenty-first Century Style

If you are a journalist the chances are close to 100 percent that someone has tried to manipulate you. Your source in a grand theft case, for example, may have selfish reasons for confiding in you but it's unlikely he makes a career of manipulating the media. He wants to nail his boss or the company he believes ruined him. Professional manipulators, on the other hand, seek to persuade a wary, hostile, skeptical, or open-minded newspaper, magazine, or broadcast station to view them and their clients in a favorable light. It's called "spin." It's practiced by politicians, corporate executives, educational institutions, world leaders, charitable organizations, think tanks, the military, and countless other entities. Spin has developed to the point that a book has been written about it: *Spin—How to Turn the Power of the Press to Your Advantage* (Regnery, 1998). Its author, Michael S. Sitrick, chief executive of a public relations firm with offices in New York and Los Angeles, describes his mission this way: "The successful spin doctor gets the press to *want* to go where he likes it to go."

A *New Yorker* cartoon shows a business executive reading a document apparently containing bad news for his company. He says to his aides: "Has our apologist been alerted?"

Of course, the spinner is not assured of success. News organizations with experienced and well-trained editors and reporters may print or air the position being put forth but will balance it with the results of their own investigation, as well as hearing from the other side. Reporters going away from an interview or news conference tend not to take the presentation and the press-kit material at face value. They may not use it at all and, if they do, other voices will be sought on the subject. Still, there are many P.R. people and their employers who earn their high salaries by pushing their position before the media. Planes crash, products turn out to be faulty and dangerous, a new housing development is built on sinking sand, three football stars are arrested for rape, a newly appointed White House aide is found to have a criminal past. In each case, a professional spinner faces the media with the intent of making the best of a bad situation. As noted earlier, spinners operated almost hourly in the Florida vote clash.

Spinning "is being done more and more with scientific manipulation by professional image makers and thought controllers," says Stuart Loory, a veteran newsman and a University of Missouri journalism professor. Writing in IPI (International Press Institute) *Report* magazine, Loory goes on: "This is a problem not only in election coverage but throughout a range of issues dominating the news of the day. . . . In each of these issues, coverage by the news business is heavily influenced by the controlled release of information."

Sometimes spinners go to absurd lengths to gloss over failures or improvise when there are no real developments in an issue. A meeting in Washington between former president Bill Clinton and Palestinian leader Yasser Arafat produced no significant results in reaching a Middle East peace settlement. Yet, a White House spokesman, straining to put the rosiest hue he could on the talk, told reporters: "When the chairman (Arafat) comes here, his meeting with the president is always constructive, and it is always helpful when we can help them understand" Israel's side of the dispute. To the media, that observation falls under the heading of "no news" even though such a meeting itself will be reported but not on the front page. When the parley ultimately failed to reach an accord, however, it did again become front-page news and the respective spin doctors went to work. Each, of course, blamed the other side for the failure. The White House put its own spin on the collapse.

Another notable spin job occurred when then-presidential candidate George W. Bush, in a moment of apparent confusion, seemed in doubt as to whether Social Security is a government program. Critics pounced on the gaffe. They said a potential president of the United States should know better and questioned his overall knowledge of government. Bush's media aides called a quick news conference to assert that the Texas governor was victim to a slip of the tongue and that, of course, he knew where Social Security belonged. Earlier, Bush provoked another round of ridicule when he referred to Greeks as "grecians." That, too, brought out his spinners, who played down the remark as a simple mistake. Press reps for Bush's opponent, then-Vice President Al Gore, also had a fire to put out when Gore appeared to suggest that he had invented the Internet. The corrected version was that Gore had been instrumental in boosting the Internet.

But don't be too hard on P.R. practitioners. They're doing their job, which means being loyal to their employers. Usually if nothing happens at a conference, truly professional spokespersons don't invent news. The next day, perhaps, a press secretary may have a Page 1 breakthrough in a diplomatic stalemate to share with the media. A corporate spokesperson is often able to persuade superiors to open up to the press in connection with a major story.

Spinning is not necessarily sinister or against the public interest. In fact, it may be beneficial, as in the Tylenol case. Several years ago, Tylenol was taken off store shelves around the nation after an unknown person or persons slipped poisonous tablets into some Tylenol containers and returned them to the store. Three people died after ingesting the pills. Tylenol's manufacturer, Johnson & Johnson, on the advice of its P.R. staff, chose to be upfront about the disaster. It announced it was taking the pain killer out of circulation and warned the public not to use the Tylenol it had at home. The company detailed the extent of the crime and the steps it was taking to avoid future tragedy. Likewise, Firestone quickly offered to replace thousands of defective tires free after it was discovered that faulty rubber allegedly had caused several accidents, some with loss of life. Public relations advice probably played a big part in the company's decision.

Nevertheless, be careful about swallowing anything whole, whatever the source. The late Red Smith, considered one of the greatest sportswriters of all time, relates in Jerome Holtsman's book *No Cheering in the Press Box* (Henry Holt, 1995) that sports promoters are prone to hyperbole, if not outright lying, in interviews, and adds: "The sportswriter learns to adjust, to make allowances. When you're listening to these people, who are serving special interests, you simply adjust by taking a little off the top." Ex-*Washington Post* editor Ben Bradlee states: "I hate this word 'spinning.' It's a nice, uptown way of saying 'lying.'"

Still, it must be kept in mind that no matter what drives the spinner, what he says may be news. Take his words down, evaluate them, and determine if they need confirmation or reaction from opponents or authorities on the subject. The pronouncement may turn out to be old or recycled news. It's always a smart idea before an interview to reach into your publication's "morgue" or library to see what already has been published on the matter. Says Joseph Galloway: "Don't begin an interview totally ignorant of the subject you are asking about. You must know enough to ask intelligent questions and to make certain you are getting intelligent answers." Galloway recommends that journalists not immediately interrupt sources who veer off the track during an interview. "Follow along for awhile and listen carefully," he urges. "You generally learn more on sidetrips initiated by the subject than you might expect."

His words are a good argument for not going to an interview with a preconceived idea of what you will encounter. An entertainer with a bawdy reputation may write serious poetry on the side and wants to tell you about it. A tough cop, who is feared by gang members for his relentless pursuit of them, might grow competition-quality roses. In his interview with comedian Jerry Lewis for *The New Yorker,* James Kaplan learned that Lewis also is an inventor. He developed the "video assist" that allows a director to observe a take on a miniature monitor as it is being filmed, a device widely used in movie making. If talents, special interests, or hobbies are not volunteered by the subject, dig for them with approaches like, "How do you relax with such a hectic job?" In an interview with the owner of a small but elegant Italian hotel for a travel article, this author admired a painting on the wall of his office. The hotelier shyly revealed that he was the artist. Further questioning disclosed that he was a highly recognized painter in

Italy, whose works had been displayed at top galleries in Rome and Milan. Not only was this fact folded into the story, but one of the accompanying photos showed the man at his easel.

Another example of the surprises that can emerge from an interview lies in a *Newsweek* article about coach Phil Jackson's handling of the Los Angeles Lakers basketball team. Among the oddities: Jackson leads the team in meditation and hands out books on philosophy and other subjects to players.

In his interviewing, AP editor and reporter Chuck Bartels says he usually injects the question, "What's new?"

"Obviously, I don't spring this on someone whose home was just pancaked by a tornado, but it can draw out unusual answers from sources you thought you knew," he explains. One unexpected answer came from a city manager, who announced that he had just acquired the last Roman coin he needed to complete his collection. Then, continues Bartels, there was the small-town police chief in Florida whose hobby, he revealed, was riding old wooden roller coasters.

"This also calls to mind the question I wish I had asked," Bartels went on. "There was an old fellow who hung around a mission for companionship and would turn up at government meetings to complain about whatever was on his mind. When he died, my paper ran an obit in which it was reported that he had been a World War I hero and a distinguished government servant in his day. No one had volunteered to me or anyone else at the paper that this tolerated man was really a beloved figure."

Reporters covering local government frequently have occasion to interview gadflies, who usually appear at every city council meeting, for example, to air real or imagined grievances. In some communities they are regarded as pests and given short shrift at a meeting, if any shrift at all. Probing into the background of such individuals could result in good-copy surprises. By the same token, newspapers and broadcast stations often get what are labeled "crank calls." Many do fall into that category, but if you get such a call on your phone, listen, at least for a few minutes, before you write him or her off as a crank. Murders have been solved and missing persons found through such communication.

A Question of Payment

Is there ever justification for paying a source for an interview? The answer is a flat no. Mainstream editors and reporters shudder at the idea and if they don't, they should. Barring some supermarket tabloids that do pay for particular interviews, the abiding rule in the newsroom is that, "We don't pay for news." News organizations occasionally will write a check to a consultant, but not to persons involved in events. If word gets out—and it likely will—that someone was paid for his information, the story is tainted.

Some sources will ask for money. The reporter's response should be that neither he nor his employers believe in paying for information because it is unethical to do so. Still, reports abound that payoffs have been made. Some foreign correspondents in Third World countries are said to have dealt with professional tipsters, who earn part of their living by getting paid for information. The practice, however, usually does not extend to official sources.

Even when you refuse a request for payment, the incident should be reported to your supervisor. At the least, you will have an excuse for not getting the interview. And it's also possible that the individual will talk to you without any inducement, principally because he has something to gain from it.

Ethics by Code?

A few years ago, David Flint, chairman of the executive council of the World Association of Press Councils, proposed an international code of ethics for the media as a means of enhancing the stature of journalism and adding strength to the cause of a free press. The idea was spurned by journalistic organizations, including the American Society of Newspaper Editors, the World Press Freedom Committee, the World Editors Forum, and even SPJ, which has its own code of ethics. They argued that such international strictures actually are a danger to press freedom in that they could become quasi-legal rules enforced or overseen by governments.

Their response was not unexpected. American editors and reporters particularly are wary of any press oversight that might bring in "Big Brother." UNESCO, the United Nations Educational, Scientific, and Cultural Organization, sought for years to band countries in a universal code of ethics. The notion was generally embraced by the then-Soviet Union and Third World nations but flatly rejected by Western democracies. In the United States, a national press council failed in the 1970s, largely because it did not receive the support of major newspapers like *The New York Times* and *Washington Post.* It was feared that the council could morph into a quasi-government body.

For ethical guidance, today's journalist need only examine his or her conscience or their news organization's statement of ethical standards. If none exists, they should consult their editors for guidance in fuzzy situations. Many decisions, however, are an easy call as noted earlier in the chapter: Reporters should not accept gifts or favors of value, betray sources, invent facts, and should at all times strive for accuracy, fairness, and balance.

Above all, treat your sources fairly and honestly. It will pay off in getting better stories and firming up your professional reputation. "Be straight with sources," urged Tiffany Montgomery and Dana Point of *The* (Boise) *Idaho Statesman* in a report at a Freedom Forum conference. "Be honest. If you are not going to run something, tell people why. Be genuine. People love to talk about themselves and matters that are important to them. . ."

Beat reporters were given this advice at the conference by Steve Silberman of the same newspaper: "Gain people's trust. Be honest but get to know the people on your beat better. Spend time listening to them and getting to know them."

10

Cleaning It All Up

The urge to start writing following an interview is almost irresistible. The words and images are fresh in your mind; you're pumped up at the idea of getting a Page 1 byline or a cover story in a magazine. You might even have worked out the lead in your head as you were driving back home or to the office. If you are writing for a newspaper your deadline time is much closer, although certain feature stories and series allow for greater latitude. But in either case, don't rush into print until you're sure everything is in place.

Get Your Notes in Order

Before writing, review your notes and listen to the tape if the interview was recorded. Does it all make sense? Is there a logical sequence in what was said? Are there gaps that should be filled in with further questions? Were your questions on target? Are there vague words on the tape that must be checked against your notes? Remember about background noises.

One method for making the actual writing easier is to list the material on 4X6 library cards in the order you plan to write the article. Another is to replay the tape and jot down the number on the counter when you come to an eye-catching quote or piece of information that will figure prominently in your story. No writer uses everything recorded in an interview.

David A. Fryxell, editorial director of *Writer's Digest,* writes in the magazine that he whips his notes into shape "before typing a word." He advises neophyte authors: "Exactly how you organize your research depends in part on its physical form. If I have notebooks full of scribblings, I'll number the notebook pages and highlight sections I'm pretty sure I'll want to use." He describes the arrangement of notecards as a "natural way" to organize data. You also can rely on your computer to store and organize information into a data bank. Back up everything on a disk, especially long articles. Still, we believe that nothing is safer than a hard copy, which can't be affected by a computer crash.

Whatever your choice, make sure you got what you went after in the interview. You may have gotten more than that but be certain you have the essential information to write an interesting and credible story. Reread each response to your questions to determine if the answers were clear and to the point. Another tack is to assume the role of the reader by asking yourself if you understand everything that was said.

Double-Check Names

Your best effort will be tarnished, as well as being blasted by editors and sources, if names are spelled wrong. If there is *any* doubt in your mind about the spelling of a name, double-check it with sources, the phone book, documents you may have taken away from the interview, public relations material, and so on, or any references you have on hand or can find in a library. The old adage, "Say what you like about me but spell my name right" carries a lot of truth. A source is more likely to complain about a wrong spelling of his name than anything in the content of your article—unless, of course, he is libeled. In this case, the writer will have two strikes against him or her. The author once wrote the wrong middle initial of a doctor in what otherwise was an accurate story. The physician lobbed his complaint, not at the writer, but at the newspaper's managing editor.

Also review for possible spelling errors the names of institutions, cities, streets, business firms, and any proper nouns. Your computer's spell checker or a dictionary will help you with other words that raise doubts. If you have a habit of spelling phonetically, by all means seek help. Therein lies disaster.

The Same for Numbers

There are few mistakes more devastating than leaving out a zero or adding an extra one to an article that involves money. The same is true about stores dealing with statistics. The difference between $1,000 and $1,000,000 can destroy a piece if the figures are mixed up. Fingers of shame will be pointed at the writer who reports that 5,014 people died in state traffic accidents last year instead of the correct 514. Check all numbers, currency, dates, phone numbers, percentages, listings, and so on, *very* carefully. If your piece lists ten ways to avoid sunstroke, count them to make sure there are ten. Phone numbers can be verified in the direc-

tory or by calling the number yourself. Pay particular attention to historical dates. There are many historians out
there—amateur and professional—who will jump on a mistake like a tiger on a gazelle.

Oh, Those Quotes

Taping an interview is an *almost* foolproof way to avoid a
libel action. We say "almost" because someone determined
to sue will go to court even when hearing his own voice say
the things he is denying he said. You can't prevent that but
your defense will be greatly supported by those same words.
Still, all quotes, whether taped or written (especially those
written) should be examined before you start writing—and
again when you have finished. And be sure that a quote,
however striking, is not used out of context, possibly distorting the subject's meaning.

A word of caution: there is a risk in calling a source to
confirm a quote. The risk is that he or she will quibble over
the content of your notes or on tape, or at least some of it.
They handed out the quote freely in the interview but now
have second thoughts and want to modify it or kill it. The
change will most likely dilute its impact and perhaps render
it useless. If you must call regarding your notes, paraphrase
the quote and ask if it represents his thoughts on the matter. You may still get an argument, but don't change his
phrasing if you're convinced it stands up and will strengthen
your piece. Of course, if he want to offer an even stronger
quote, don't discourage him.

Going back to a source to confirm facts is another matter.
By all means do it if there is any doubt. It can save later

trouble and the source will appreciate your professionalism. In the process, however, disclose only the facts in question. Allowing him to read your entire piece can lead to grief should he decide to become your editor, not a rare occurrence.

If a source has attributed controversial or damaging statements to other persons, the latter should be contacted for verification. Not only is this good journalism but you might get great additional grist for your story.

Who Else?

Often, you can make your piece more compelling by balancing it out with sources perhaps not mentioned by your original source. A medical article on a new drug, for example, may call for the opinions of other doctors and pharmacologists. A piece on overseas adoption can benefit from the views of various experts in the field as well as adopting parents. A politician's plan for a light rail system may draw all kinds of opposition. A much-debated national issue, a proposed missile defense system, has drawn support and criticism from a myriad of sources that cross party lines in Congress. In covering this story, a reporter after, say, getting the view of the president of the United States or the Army chief of staff, should interview a spectrum of people for a well-rounded story and not only big names. In the 2000 presidential elections, newspapers, magazines, and television fell over each other in interviewing focus groups, coffee klatch members, and cafe patrons in small towns across America. What they often got—and what you will get—are pungent, down-home quotes that enliven a story and give it added meaning. An example was an elderly Oregon woman who told the *Los Angeles Times* that she opted to see a movie rather than watch the candidates debate on television, remarking, "I watched the other debate and I'm not really crazy about either of them." A companion in the coffee shop added: "They're both idiots." Still another commented that he paid no attention to the debates but would vote for Vice President Al Gore because he felt he would be a winner. Rarely will such citizens refuse to talk to a reporter. They may not admit it but they usually are flattered that someone really cares about their opinion.

And don't forget the library and the Internet as sources for obtaining missing pieces. This process will go much easier if you know exactly what you want. Most libraries these days have gone well beyond card catalogues and can serve up information in quick order. Some may even have a bank of computers for public use. Bookstores, too, can come up with the volume you want by merely tapping into a computer. Be prepared to pay for copies of articles. Some stories may require your using the Freedom of Information Act to obtain information from government sources.

Don't Dump Those Notes

Hold on to your notes and tapes for at least three months. If there is a question or complaint about your article, they will be your defense. Moreover, the notes may contain information that could be the kernel of another magazine or newspaper article. Deborah J. Myers Post, in a *Writer's Digest* article, recalls that she once sold a piece on home-schooling to *At-Home Mothering* and then queried an article on the same topic with a different angle to an educational trade magazine.

Material collected for a travel article should be kept forever. For example, a piece on the cluster of antique shops in one section of Buenas Aires might initially be written as just one aspect of shopping in that city. Why not then pitch it to *Antique Review* or another magazine specializing in antiques, slanting it toward an audience with a sophisticated knowledge? Cindy Yorks, the California writer, recalls that information collected for one article led to sales in four other publications.

It should be noted here that retaining notes, tapes, and broadcast outtakes from news interviews is a subject for debate in journalism circles. Some attorneys for newspapers and broadcast stations advise that material gleaned from interviews should be tossed out as soon as possible. They argue that plaintiffs' lawyers in a libel suit can subpoena the notes to prove their case. Some editors agree with the advice and some don't. The latter contend that if a reporter has done a professional job, and if he or she has a record of accuracy, the notes will boost the defense. Tapes and outtakes normally speak for themselves but it may be claimed that the printed or broadcast version took quotes out of context or that there was a deliberate attempt to confuse the source with trick questions.

Harold W. Fuson Jr., vice president and chief legal officer of Copley Press, a newspaper chain, advises reporters to maintain a "clean desk" by regularly getting rid of notes that are no longer useful and which might be subpoenaed in a criminal or civil trial. An exception, the lawyer notes, might be made for beat reporters and others covering a story on a continuing basis, who maintain files on certain individuals or issues. Generally, however, notes "have a very limited lifespan," he contends.

The final stages of your interview also may involve assuring your source that he or she will get a fair shake. Be straight with them if the question comes up. State plainly that your article will be edited and that cuts or changes may be made because of space limitations or other reasons—that it may not even be published. But also stress that you will do everything you can to preserve the integrity of the piece by a fair and truthful presentation of his statements. And then do it. Some editors will discuss proposed changes with writers. If yours doesn't, ask to see page proofs of an article that embodies controversy or is of a delicate nature. Don't be afraid to argue against editing that distorts your story. If a source feels he has been wronged, his blame will fall on you, not on the editor.

Editors, alas, win most of the disputes with writers, although some are willing to compromise. This is not to say that editors are always wrong—the bad guys. While the reporter may be passionately wrapped up in his story to the point of seeing no flaws in it, the editor is in a position to take a detached view, bringing in his or her experience to possibly save the writer from making a serious misjudgment—or to stave off a libel action. Several staff writers, including Pulitzer Prize-winners, can thank city editors and/or copy editors for successful stories. Their contribution can include removing excess baggage, subbing stronger verbs, untangling twisted syntax, and smoothing out the continuity.

The late essayist E. B. White observed: "An editor is a person who knows more about writing than writers do but who has escaped the terrible desire to write."

A less kind assessment of editors was voiced by an unknown scribe who said: "An editor separates the wheat from the chaff and then throws away the wheat."

Let's hope that your editor falls into E. B. White's evaluation. But if you're writing for a magazine or newspaper, it's likely that more than one editor will review your work. Still, your own careful editing should be an automatic process with any copy. If rewrite, all or in part, is necessary, do it. Straighten out those awkward sentences, get rid of those wrong words, eliminate unneeded adjectives, dump unnecessary flourishes, and erase anything that sounds like an opinion or point of view—unless you're writing a column, editorial, or analysis. Consider also how much your audience may already know so you won't bore them with warmed-over material. There's a fine line here. You can't depend on the casual reader knowing the background of a story so some background is usually indicated. Just don't carry it too far. Television and radio usually supply little or no background, being primarily a headline service, but print journalists are expected to properly frame a story. Look carefully at newspaper stories to learn how the writers wove in background at the proper place.

Summing Up

1. Examine your notes carefully. Do they make sense? Do they enhance the story? Do you need to get additional quotes?
2. Do you have enough material for a balanced, cohesive story?
3. Are all your sources treated fairly?
4. Are the names spelled right and the titles correct?
5. Did you get what you went after?

11

Writing It All Down

As soon as you're done with your interviews, transcribe your notes. If you wait, you're less likely to be able to read the chicken scrawl that passes for your handwriting. Sometimes, on breaking news stories, when you're interviewing, reporting, and writing within a day's time, transcribing your notes is often unnecessarily time-consuming. But if you know you'll be doing lots of interviews and waiting a few days or a few weeks to write your story, you'd be well advised to get as much of your notes typed out as soon as possible.

How do you know when you're done interviewing and ready to write?

1. When you've run out of time
2. When sources are beginning to say the same things
3. When you're absolutely certain you understand the problem completely and have spoken to everyone who can help you understand it better

If you've reached point three, it's time to think, not write.

Reporters who fail to organize their thinking usually end up with a disorganized, unfocused story. Many reporters believe when they sit down to write the story, some divine inspiration will guide them. For a lucky few blessed with native story-telling abilities, writing is effortless and always well done. For just about everyone else, writing without thinking results in a muddled mess. Here's how to avoid that mess and create a well-organized, compelling, and easy-to-read finished product for newspapers, magazines, or television.

Finding Your Focus

Throughout the reporting process, you have created, reevaluated, and changed your focus repeatedly as the story twisted and turned in different directions. At some point in your reporting, you should have fixed on an approach or a theme and discussed it with your editor. Now is the time to refine that focus and tell your editor what angle you'll pursue when writing the story. Does your editor agree with it? If your editor doesn't agree, better to argue it out now, before you turn the story in on deadline and precipitate the sort of crisis that is rarely resolved the way a reporter wants it to be. Maybe you're confused or so close to your story you've forgotten to ask a crucial question. A good editor will assist you, but you have to ask for help directly.

"Ms. Editor, I have all this information but I'm not sure what the story's focus is. Can you help me find it?"

Your editor should ask you a series of questions that will eventually give you direction, a sentence that sums up the single most important point you're trying to make. If you can't boil down your story to one sentence, you haven't thought hard enough. If you've thought as hard as your brain will allow and you're still unclear, it might mean you need to do more reporting, that you still don't understand the story. Go back to your sources and ask more questions until the single sentence emerges. Sometimes it's helpful to ask yourself a few questions. "What was the most important or unusual thing that happened?" "What do I want to say about it?" Once you've done that, ask yourself: "Who cares?" and "So what?" When you and your editor are satisfied with your response, you've found your focus. Now you have to organize the rest of your story.

Good Writing Is Good Thinking

Many reporters refuse to organize stories before they write, preferring to struggle first for the perfect lead, expecting "the rest of the story will flow like lava," writes the Portland *Oregonian*'s writing guru Jack Hart in *Editor & Publisher.* These reporters, Hart says, often discover that:

- Writing is agony. For writers who have no guideposts to lead them through confusing material, progress can be painfully slow. Every story degenerates into a stressful series of false starts, detours, and wasted time.
- Their stories are repetitious. Because no grand scheme guides the placement of material, the same points show up again and again.
- The good stuff gets cut. Color dropped into a disorganized story as an afterthought is an easy cut for a harried editor.
- Quality trails off after the opening.

- They waste a lot of time and mental resources as they move blocks of copy, shifting material around inside the story. They end up driving themselves—and their editors—crazy.

Hart continues:

> "The failure to take time for organizing ends up wasting huge amounts of time in the writing. The act of writing down a theme statement and a few main topics imposes on the chaos of detail you often face when reporting ends. It relieves panic because it allows you to ease into the story.
>
> Writing is thinking. That's all there is to it. Simple as it is, it still works wonders."

Clustering

Clustering is a useful thinking tool. Here's how it works:

1. Put away your notes.

   Resist temptation to refer to your notes. You know a lot more than you think you do.
2. Cast your story's focus as a single-sentence statement.

   This may seem simple, but with complicated stories, it might take you as much as an hour to figure out that single sentence.

   To assist you in constructing the sturdiest possible focus, we offer a few suggestions. First, cast your story's focus in terms of actors and action. Who's doing what to whom? Use action verbs to craft the focus, no static "to be" verbs or passive voice.

3. In the middle of a piece of paper, write down your focus statement and draw a circle around it. Imagine your circle as a wheel and draw spokes coming out from it.

   At the end of each spoke, draw a smaller circle. In each of the circles, write down one of the many aspects of your story that relates to the focus. Anytime you get stuck, analyze your focus statement and ask yourself: "So what?" "Who cares?" As you fill in your cluster, do it randomly, drawing as many spokes and circles as you have information to illuminate the focus. Connect the circles that are related. Keep doing it until you feel certain you've put down on paper every aspect of the story and you've noted how the various parts of the story relate to one another.

   When the cluster is completed, use the information to create an outline. Pay careful attention to how you craft the top of the story. Make sure it answers who, what, when, where, why, and how. If the story is a feature, profile, news-feature, or trend piece, make sure it has a strong focus statement in the first few paragraphs, along with a news hook, background, and strong quote that illuminates the focus.

Outlines

Spot news stories—also called breaking news stories—usually follow a standard formula for writing called the inverted pyramid. Using the inverted pyramid formula means organizing your information so that the most important goes first, the least important last. (Think of an upside-down triangle, with the broad base at the top, the pointed end at the bottom. The broad base represents the most important information; the pointed end represents the least important.)

Before you begin writing, create an outline. Just as you would never get on the freeway for a cross-country drive without consulting a map, you should never embark on a story without a plan. The outline is the road map you'll use to figure out the easiest, quickest way to your destination.

The outline for a spot news story contains the following elements:

- Lead (1–2 paragraphs)
  - Sums up the focus of your story
  - Orients readers by telling them something surprising; entices them to continue reading for more details
  - Answers the questions Who? What? When? Where? Why? How?—ordering the information from most important to least important
- Background (1 paragraph)
- Impact (Who will be hurt? Helped?) (1 paragraph)
- Reaction and response from critics or supporters (1 paragraph)
- Cosmic quote that illuminates the story's focus (1 paragraph)
- Explanation of lead, including facts, quotes, anecdotes and other evidence used to support the issues introduced in the lead. Remember to use parallel construction when writing the rest of the story.

Now go through your notes and identify the facts, figures, quotes and anecdotes, you need to fully explain the story's focus, its impact, and the reaction it engendered. Though we're providing you with guidelines, your story will dictate what information goes where. Sometimes the cosmic quote will follow the background paragraph; sometimes the reaction will precede the impact. Not all stories contain all these elements, although most do. If you think reporting the reaction to your story's focus is irrelevant, you may be right. But be prepared to justify to your editor why you failed to include it.

Clear Writing Reflects Clear Thinking

How do you know what to put in the story and what to leave out? The question answers itself if you've created an outline. Leave out any information that fails to advance the story's focus. Often, after organizing their notes, reporters realize they spent a great deal of time collecting interesting yet irrelevant information and still need to do more reporting to clearly explain their story's focus. The outline finds the story's holes quickly. It also identifies information potentially useful for a sidebar.

A sidebar to a story explores an issue or idea that, while interesting, fails to fit into the main story because it remains tangential to the focus. Sidebars engage readers by giving them more information if they want it, helping to draw them into the issues of the main story. Decide with your editor at the outline stage what information you want to put into the main story and what you'd like in a sidebar.

On Writing Well

Though stylistic differences exist between journalism and other sorts of writing, certain truths still apply. Some of those truths include these basic rules:

1. Cut unnecessary fat.

    "If I had more time," Mark Twain once wrote to a friend, "I would have written you a shorter letter." Twain believed in conveying the greatest meaning with the fewest words, and so should you. Preserve meaning, but prune ruthlessly.

2. Use simple, clear language. Stories lose their punch when they contain vague, mushy adjectives. Stick to strong nouns and verbs that describe actors and action. The following examples show how to sharpen your focus.

    Fuzzy: His head was injured by a blunt instrument.
    Clear: An unidentified attacker fractured his skull with a sledgehammer.
    Fuzzy: The chief executive rode down the main thoroughfare.
    Clear: Gov. Paulson rode down Spencer Avenue in a convertible BMW.
    Fuzzy: Officers removed a gun from his clothing.
    Clear: Police took a .32-caliber revolver from his pocket.

3. Say what you mean.
    What's wrong here:

    The divers strapped on oxygen tanks, jumped into the water and began searching the swollen river for the body of the lost heiress.
    Divers breathe air, not oxygen. When in doubt, look it up.

What's wrong here:

The controversy centers around the ongoing battle between the Republicans, who want less government spending, and the Democrats, who want to preserve assistance programs for the poor.

It's not possible to "center around"; the controversy "centers on."

What's wrong here:

Over 150 people attended the conference, which drew delegates from as far away as Africa and Asia.

"Over" does not mean "more than."

What's wrong here:

Hopefully, Charles Whitcomb will remain in prison for the rest of his life, said June Thompson, the woman he was convicted of raping.

Unless Whitcomb is serving his sentence "full of hope," the word "hopefully" is misused.

4. Choose active over passive voice.

Wherever possible, replace static "to be" verbs ("there is," "is going," "will have gone," etc.) with action verbs. Be careful not to confuse tense with voice.

Passive voice: The money was owed by him.
Active voice: He owed the money.
Passive voice: A lot of prizes were won by the couple in the lottery.
Active voice: The couple won a lot of prizes in the lottery.

5. Craft transitions carefully.

Transitions—a few words or a sentence—act as a bridge linking related but different ideas. The most commonly used transitions are chronological (now, since, then, a few days later, etc.) and conjunctions (and, but, then, however, etc.).

Instead of crafting appropriate transitions, beginning writers often rely on attributions to move the reader from one thought to the next. Avoid misusing attributions as transitions.

6. Replace cliches and adjectives with nouns and action verbs focusing on actors and action.

Over the years, TV news viewers and newspaper readers have come to expect politicians to toss their hats in the ring, prisoners to hear sentences without visible emotion, and state legislatures to work against the clock to pass bills. Any figure of speech that you're used to seeing in print or any word or phrase that springs easily to mind is a cliche. Writers avoid cliches by looking for fresh words and images and by recasting cliches to focus on actors and action.

> He was caught by the long arm of the law.
> Police officers arrested him.

> The mayor is a veteran campaigner.
> The mayor faces his fifth campaign, the most contentious yet.

> Bancroft was an outspoken critic of the school board.
> Bancroft often criticized the school board.

> The council grappled with the issue for several hours.
> Council members discussed the issue for several hours, rarely agreeing.

> Police scoured the neighborhood.
> Police officers searched the neighborhood.

7. Translate jargon by paraphrasing dull, wordy quotes.

Let's say test scores at the local high school are way down and you're assigned to find out why.

The principal tells you: "Our challenge is to consider the recent impact of the influx of differently-abled and economically challenged students in our district and to launch a course of action exploring the possibility that this recent variation in the student demographic probably influenced the previously unforeseen declivity in academic achievement."

Your challenge: to translate this bureaucratic nonsense into English. This is actually what the principal is saying: "A recent, large increase in the number of poor and disabled students coming into the district may have contributed to declining test scores."

8. Use quotes correctly.

Quotes in stories are like exclamation marks at the ends of sentences or punch lines of jokes. They should illuminate, support, and surprise.

In a well-organized story, quotes fall into place easily and never require clumsy explanation. Instead of writing: "If they had told us ahead of time, we would have stayed home and not wasted all this money," said Rina Fox, referring to the family's recent trip to the Beaver Town amusement park and the fact that they were unable to enter the park because officials failed to publicize the two-day shutdown for remodeling.

Set up the quote as you would the punch line to a joke:

Beaver Town officials ruined the plans of many families—some had come from as far away as Des

Moines—by failing to publicize the amusement park's recent two-day shutdown for remodeling. "If they had told us ahead of time, we would have stayed home and not wasted all this money," said Rina Fox, her two disappointed children by her side.

- Try to avoid quoting people who speak in expected cliches or say the obvious, such as the coach who tells you, "We won because we played real well."
- Unless you're re-creating dialogue, avoid bumping quotes, the practice of following one person's quote with another person's quote. Instead, use a transition to separate quotes.
- Follow basic rules of usage. This is incorrect: "'I couldn't be happier,' he grinned." A grin doesn't speak. "'I couldn't be happier,' he said, grinning." Much better. The same holds true for: "'I couldn't be happier,' he smiled." "'I couldn't be happier,' he said, smiling" is correct usage.

9. Prefer the concrete to the abstract. If you must introduce an abstract concept, make sure you explain it with a concrete example. This is especially true of the following:

- Numbers. If you say the county lost $2 billion in a bad investment scheme, tell your readers what that means: "Officials lost $2 billion in a bad investment scheme, enough money to house every homeless family in the county for 25 years."
- Abstract nouns: What is a facility? An issue? A problem? They mean different things to different people. If "the facility" is a factory where workers assemble circuit boards, say so.

- Adjectives: As Mark Twain once said, "When you catch an adjective, kill it." Adjectives are subjective. You and an Eskimo have different understandings of "cold," just as you and an unemployed single father living on welfare with five kids in a one-bedroom apartment have different understandings of "posh." Stick to factual descriptions based on the details you've gathered in your reporting.

  Instead of using "posh" to describe the accommodations, write: "The delegates, assembled to discuss ways to abolish welfare, will spend the weekend at a five-star hotel with gold-plated sinks, ocean views and a $400-a-day price tag."

On Journalistic Style

Now we move to the specifics of journalistic style. Most journalists work with a basic set of guidelines. As you craft your stories, pay careful attention to the following:

1. Attributions

   Any fact or opinion that isn't widely accepted must be attributed to a source. (Examples of widely accepted facts: The earth revolves around the sun, or a week has seven days.)

   Attributions almost always go at the end of the sentence unless who's saying something is more important than what's being said.

   - Avoid loaded words.
   - Instead of writing "he admitted," stick to "he said." It conveys less judgment on the writer's part. A well-crafted story lets the facts speak for themselves.

- Never attribute a single quote to more than one person unless people are speaking in unison.
- Cut any unattributed opinion from your story.
- Statistics and numbers should be paraphrased and attributed to their proper source.

2. Tone

Journalists tend to write in the third person and use a conversational tone. Imagine as you write that you're telling the story to someone you know well, your mom or a best friend, for example.

3. Language

- Avoid acronyms.

    Unless acronyms are well known—CIA or FBI, for example—never use them. Even with CIA or FBI, you must tell the reader what the acronym stands for on first reference.

    Let's say you're writing about a philosophical change in the Department of English and Comparative Literary Studies curriculum.

    A beginning journalist might write:

    The Department of English and Comparative Literary Studies (ECLS) at Knowitall University (KU) will offer fewer courses focusing on white male authors.

    With the approval of the KU provost, the ECLS department will refocus its curriculum to offer courses featuring women, minority and gay and lesbian writers, which angers many in the more traditional School of the Humanities and Fine Arts (SHFA).

"We think this makes up for years gone by when we didn't offer a single course with a female, minority, gay or lesbian voice," said ECLS department chair Joseph Book.

But not all agreed. SHFA officials denounced ECLS professors and accused KU of favoring the department of ECLS over the SHEA.

Simplify the story by deleting the acronyms. On first reference, identify the departments by their correct names. On second reference, refer simply to the English department, the university, the humanities school.

- Avoid sexist and racist assumptions.

Some commonly misused references to gender include housewife or househusband, which implies a woman or man is married to the house. Homemaker more accurately describes a woman or man who works in the home.

Use of the word man to describe an important position—chairman, councilman, congressman—excludes large numbers of women who fill these posts. Change references to make them gender neutral: for example, chair of the committee, city council member and member of Congress.

Use a person's race, religion, or sexual orientation only when relevant to the story—for instance when describing a fugitive from the law or a controversy that centers on race or gender. If a black executive was denied membership in an all-white country club, race would be discussed in the story. But if a Latino teen was arrested on suspicion of embezzling funds from the campus yearbook account, his race is irrelevant. (You would never write, for instance: "A white teenager was arrested Tuesday for embezzling funds from the campus yearbook account.")

4. Focus on people and their stories

Bureaucrats love to speak abstractly. For instance, one might say: "The American people support our plan to save their hard-earned tax dollars by ending federal handouts like welfare and Medicare."

What does that mean? Explain it by focusing on the people most affected: tell their stories and open the window on their world for your readers or viewers. Find the single mother with three children living in a homeless shelter and show what cutting welfare means to those who depend on it. Or find a senior citizen who forgoes meat to pay for the medicine he needs because his Medicare benefits were cut.

5. The ending: crafting the kicker

Try to end gracefully, usually with a quote. At the very least, avoid ending on an attribution. The following ending to a story about two Los Angeles high school crosstown football rivals leaves the reader with a sense of finality:

"The Banning coach is sending out a false message about Los Angeles that you can't even attend a football game without being afraid of losing your life," said City Councilman Nate Holden, who represents the Dorsey area. "Banning has nothing to fear but losing the game."

A less-skillful writer might have ended the story on an attribution:

"The Banning coach is sending out a false message about Los Angeles that you can't even attend a football game without being afraid of losing your life. Banning has nothing to fear but losing the game," said City Councilman Nate Holden, who represents the Dorsey area.

Well-told endings are sometimes called "kickers" because they give the reader a little kick or surprise. Save a particularly funny quote or an unexpected detail for the end of your story to leave readers with a sense of finality.

Editors, readers, and viewers will judge your story on its reporting as well as its writing. Writers without solid reporting won't have the necessary information to carry out their mandate. As you craft your stories, anticipate readers' or viewers' questions. Ask yourself: How much will it cost my readers? What will my readers get out of it? How will it affect my readers? Why should my readers care?

The Importance of Accuracy

Your story's reporting will be judged on two criteria: Is it accurate? Is it fair? Accuracy means you got the facts straight and you spelled the names correctly. Factual errors leave your publication or TV station open to a libel lawsuit, an expense media owners would rather forego.

Even a few factual errors call into question the veracity of the entire story. In an article for the *Columbia Journalism Review,* author Alicia Mundy described the strategy P.R. firms use when reporters report stories unflattering to their clients: "Attack any and all flaws in a reporter's story, then use them to discredit the whole piece." "(The) philosophy is: If you get (reporters) to back down on the minor details they've screwed up on, they're unlikely to fight you on the major ones."

To ensure your piece is accurate, double-check every fact you use against your notes. Whenever possible, call back sources to confirm statistics and anecdotes. Make sure you always ask sources to spell their names and tell you their correct titles, even when it seems obvious.

Rarely read back quotes, though, since it gives the source an opportunity to censor what was said. It is possible—and desirable—to double-check the correct spelling of names, titles, dates, and other facts you use in the quotes.

The Art of Self-Editing

Once finished writing the story, writers often believe the work before them is a masterpiece. It isn't. You've just created the rough draft. Now comes the hard part. If you haven't already, check your ego at the door. You must assess your work critically, dispassionately, as an editor or a reader would. Imagine as you review the story that you're reading it for the first time. This is often difficult, especially since you've likely become close to the subject and lack the distance needed to ferret out a story's weaknesses. But remember: Constructive criticism improves the work and has nothing to do with you as a human being or your potential as a writer. For you and your editor, the goal is singular: to create the best story in as little time as possible. That means you may get scant encouragement from editors more concerned with polishing a diamond in the rough than attending to your feelings. In fact, after a careful editor works over your story, you may decide to pursue a career that involves no writing at all, like dishwashing.

Accept from the start that good editors will return your stories filled with demands for revisions and rewrites. If your story lacks those edits, then assume one of three things: (1) you are among the rare and truly gifted, a Mozart of the printed word; (2) your editor is an idiot; (3) you have perfected the art of self-editing.

Self-editing is as much a skill as writing a lead or organizing a story, and you must dedicate yourself to the discipline it requires. The first draft of your story is rarely your final draft. The first draft gets it down on paper. Now comes the rewrite.

Whenever possible and time permits, evaluate your own story for editorial soundness. Measure it against the basic guidelines we've outlined in this chapter. The following is a checklist you should use before you submit your story to an editor.

1. Lead
   - The lead clearly states the essential news of the story and answers the questions who, what, when, where, why, and how.
   - A background paragraph provides perspective, when necessary.
2. Organization
   - The story has a clear focus.
   - Evidence supporting the focus follows a logical progression.
   - Sentences are well constructed. Each relates logically to the next.

- The reader moves easily from paragraph to paragraph.
- Transitions ease readers from one issue to the next.

3. Writing
    - Active voice is used throughout.
    - Simple, clear, precise language is used throughout.
    - Writer shows, doesn't tell.
    - Unnecessary fat is cut.
    - Concrete examples explain abstract concepts.
    - Dull, wordy quotes are paraphrased.
    - Writer puts attributions at the end or middle of sentences instead of at the beginning.

4. Reporting
    - The story accurately describes the event or issue.
    - It quotes correct and appropriate sources.
    - It has no holes and is missing no important information.

5. It is free from spelling, style, and grammar errors.

Bibliography

Anderson, Rob, and George M. Killenberg. *Interviewing: Speaking, Listening and Learning for Professional Life.* Mountain View, CA: Mayfield Publishing, 1999.

Biagi, Shirley. *Interviews that Work: A Practical Guide for Journalists.* 2nd ed. Belmont, CA: Wadsworth, 1992.

Brady, John Joseph. *The Craft of Interviewing.* New York: Vintage Books, 1977.

Cohen, Akiba A. *The Television News Interview.* Newbury Park, CA: Sage, 1987.

Donaghy, William. *The Interview: Skills and Applications.* Glenview, IL: Scott, Foresman, 1984.

Douglas, Jack D. *Creative Interviewing.* Beverly Hills: Sage Publications, 1985.

Dreifus, Claudia. *Interview.* New York: Seven Stories Press, 1997.

Gordon, Raymond L. *Interviewing: Strategy, Techniques and Tactics.* Homewood, IL: The Dorsey Press, 1980.

Gottlieb, Marvin R. *Interview.* New York: Longman, 1986.

Jucker, Andreas H. *News Interviews: A Pragmalinguistic Analysis.* Philadelphia: J. Benjamins, 1986.

Killenberg, George M., and Rob Anderson. *Before the Story: Interviewing and Communication Skills for Journalists.* New York: St. Martin's Press, 1989.

McLaughlin, Paul. *Asking Questions: The Art of the Media Interview.* Vancouver, BC: International Self-Counsel Press Ltd., 1986.

McMahan, Eva M. *Interactive Oral History Interviewing.* Hillsdale, NJ: Lawrence Erlbaum, 1994.

Merman, Stephen K., and John E. McLaughlin. *Out-Interviewing the Interviewer: A Job Winner's Script for Success.* Englewood Cliffs, NJ: Prentice-Hall, 1983.

Metzler, Ken. *Creative Interviewing.* 2nd ed. Englewood Cliffs, NJ: Prentice-Hall, 1989.

Presson, Hazel. *The Student Journalist and Interviewing.* New York: R. Rosen Press, 1979.

Rafe, Stephen C. *Mastering the News Media Interview: How to Do Successful Television, Radio & Print Interviews.* New York: Harper, 1991.

Rivers, William L. *Finding Facts: Interviewing, Observing, Using Reference Sources.* Englewood Cliffs, NJ: Prentice-Hall, 1975.

Siegel, Robert, ed. *The NPR Interviews.* (Volumes 1994-1996) Boston, MA: Houghton Mifflin, 1994-1996.

Silvester, Christopher, ed. *The Norton Book of Interviews: An Anthology from 1859 to the Present Day.* London: W. W. Norton Company, 1996.

Sitzmann, Marion, and Reloy Garcia. *Successful Interviewing: A Practical Guide for the Applicant and Interviewer.* Skokie, IL: National Textbook Company, 1981.

Skopec, Eric W. *Situational Interviewing.* New York: Harper & Row, 1986.

Stein, M. L., and Susan F. Paterno. *The Newswriter's Handbook: An Introduction to Journalism.* Ames, IA: Iowa State University Press, 1998.

Stewart, Charles J., and William B. Cash. *Interviewing: Principles and Practices.* 7th ed. Dubuque, IA: W. C. Brown, 1994.

Yate, Martin John. *Knock 'em Dead: With Great Answers to Tough Interview Questions.* Boston: B. Adams, 1987.